David Schrot

CURRICULUM BASED ASSESSMENT

CURRICULUM BASED ASSESSMENT

A Primer

By

CHARLES H. HARGIS

Department of Special Education and Rehabilitation
The University of Tennessee
Knoxville, Tennessee

CHARLES C THOMAS • PUBLISHER
Springfield • Illinois • U.S.A.

Published and Distributed Throughout the World by
CHARLES C THOMAS • PUBLISHER
2600 South First Street
Springfield, Illinois 62794-9265

© *1987 by* CHARLES C THOMAS • PUBLISHER
ISBN 0-398-05288-3
Library of Congress Catalog Card Number: 86-14523

With THOMAS BOOKS *careful attention is given to all details of manufacturing and design. It is the Publisher's desire to present books that are satisfactory as to their physical qualities and artistic possibilities and appropriate for their particular use.* THOMAS BOOKS *will be true to those laws of quality that assure a good name and good will.*

Printed in the United States of America
Q-R-3

Library of Congress Cataloging in Publication Data

Hargis, Charles H.
    Curriculum based assessment.

    Bibliography: p.
    Includes index.
    1. Criterion-referenced tests — United States.
2. Educational tests and measurements — United States.
3. Learning   disabled   children — Education — United
States.
I. Title.
LB3060.32.C74H37   1987   371.2'6   86-14523
ISBN 0-398-05288-3

PREFACE

IN THIS small book, I have attempted to explain the concepts that make up curriculum-based assessment and how they work together. I have provided some illustrations on its use and made some suggestions on its implementation.

The ingredients of curriculum-based assessment are not new. Neither are its ideas at all complex. Yet, the results of the recipe that synthesizes its components are novel and, on some points, controversial. Still, I believe it represents the best way for learning disabled and low achieving students to gain adequate educational opportunity. In fact, such a program benefits all children.

The methods of assessment and instruction described herein are simple and direct. I hope they seem obvious and rational. I believe that clear, simple procedures are usually best and hope I have approached some level of clearness and simplicity in my explanation of curriculum-based assessment. This is, after all, a primer.

ACKNOWLEDGMENTS

MY THANKS to Linda Hargis for essential editorial assistance. They go also to Ed Gickling. The ideas in this book are the joint product of our long association.

CONTENTS

Page

Preface... v

Chapter

  1. Central Concepts... 3
  2. Success or Challenge...................................... 9
  3. Assessment That Is Curriculum Based...................... 15
  4. Instructional Levels and Rates in Reading 29
  5. Instructional Levels and Rates in Arithmetic............... 43
  6. Instruction with Assessment................................ 51
  7. The Preparation and Selection of Materials................. 65
  8. Identifying Learning Disabled Students..................... 81
  9. Other Assessment Concerns................................. 87
10. Administrative Support for CBA............................. 95
11. Teacher Training...103
     Charles H. Hargis and Susan Benner

References...111
Index...113

CURRICULUM BASED ASSESSMENT

CHAPTER 1

CENTRAL CONCEPTS

The Bed of Procrustes

REMEMBER Procrustes?

He was that legendary scoundrel from Attica with that horrible iron bed. Travelers who were unfortunate enough to sleep in it were either stretched to fit with a rack if too short or were shortened with an ax if too tall.

Fortunately, Theseus took care of Procrustes and his bed. Unfortunately, there is still a procrustean bed to which a group of children must fit.

This iron bed is the typical curriculum for kindergarten through high school. Routinely, student progress is measured against the curricular components of his or her particular grade. Each grade has a set of curricular objectives for each subject sequenced over the nine-month school year. The assessment procedures in use determine how the student measures up to the curricular objectives. If the student doesn't measure up, then s/he is given a failing grade. Regular failure will attract a label, usually suggesting a learning disability. Indeed, failure is the primary diagnostic procedure by which we identify learning disabled children.

Procrustes now is the school board, the administration, and the teachers who design and control the curricular beds to which they force children to fit. The axes and racks now used to fit students to these iron curricular beds are the traditional forms of assessment used to assign failure when students don't measure up. Fifteen to twenty-five percent of all students don't fit; consequently they fail.

Despite substantial learning ability, these students, who are often called learning disabled, are actually casualties of inflexible curricula.

There needs to be a modern Theseus come to slay this new Procrustes and replace his iron bed with one more generous and humane.

Curriculum-based assessment (CBA) is such a champion. It is a system used to adjust the curriculum to fit students and so eliminate such unfortunate casualties.

From an Old Idea

The notion that the curriculum is rigid is not particularly new. Emmett Betts (1936) stated that many reading problems were created simply because we do not make basic adjustments to deal with individual differences. Undoubtedly, some reading disabilities are caused when a child is required to start reading instruction before he is generally ready. Betts estimated at the time that about 15 percent of the children were so disabled. Later (1946) he elaborated on the problem, attributing it also to the "lock step" nature of school organization. Here instruction was provided based on the assumption that every child was to climb the same curriculum ladder. Objectives were set up in grade levels. Each level represented a rung on the curricular ladder. At about the same chronological age, usually 6, children took the first step, the first grade. The goal of each teacher was to prepare the class for the next grade. The grade itself was broken into units of work through which all children were to proceed. Reading programs and content areas alike were designed for these gradations or steps on the assumption that all children are capable of uniform achievement. Children who could not manage to maintain this rate of achievement might be provided with "remedial" instruction to help them achieve grade level. Those who could not keep the pace were either socially promoted or repeated the grade. The same rate of learning progress was required of all children regardless of the individual intrinsic readiness level or speed of learning.

A lot of verbage has been devoted to the importance of individual differences in instruction. However, in practice the comments of Betts seem to apply quite accurately to today's schools.

Spache (1976) said that sufficiently flexible, primary-level teachers can handle students that vary six months or so from exact grade placement. However, in the existing structure a child who functions a year or more below grade placement presents a demand for individualized instruction that the average teacher does not recognize or readily meet. Spache also pointed out that 30 percent of students above the primary grades are a year or more below grade-level placement in reading achievement.

Harris and Sipay (1975) state that 25 percent of all students need reading instruction that differs from regular reading programs. These "slow learners" require materials that proceed at a slower pace.

Jansky and de Hirsch (1972) show that teachers rated as adequate by principles had a failure rate of 23 percent of their students. However, teachers rated as poor showed a 49 percent failure rate of their children. These data strongly indicate that teachers can influence the effectiveness of reading instruction, but it is apparent that without a major adjustment in the management of the reading curriculum itself, many so-called learning disabled children will continue to be products or casualties of the curriculum.

Testing and Teaching

Too many tests in use today have too little in common with the curricular objectives of the classes where they are used. Curriculum based assessment is designed to insure that there is a correspondence between the tests or testing procedures used and the curriculum. This correspondence is necessary not only for test validity but to place low achieving (LA) and learning disabled (LD) students at a place on the curriculum where they can work successfully and make progress.

Most testing that goes on in classrooms today is for the purpose of assigning grades. But, we already know that the LA and LD students are failing; that is how they were first identified. That also remains their unfortunate lot in most classrooms. The focus of assessment must change for these children. The testing procedures should not be used to assign grades but to accurately assign a student to a level of instruction where he can succeed and achieve. Success is fundamental to CBA.

Success and Achievement

Success is certainly more than just avoiding failure, and throughout the book, more precise definitions of success in various instructional situations will be added. Fundamentally, success can be viewed as what is needed to keep a student on-task to the satisfactory completion of an instructional activity. If a task is too difficult, a student cannot remain on-task. If a task is too difficult, a student cannot pursue it to a satisfactory completion. Achievement is tied to amount of time spent on learning. Time off-task is not time engaged in learning. CBA is intended to identify tasks and activities that are doable for individual students; activities and objectives that are an appropriate level of difficulty so that these students can be rewarded by success experiences and so that they can remain on-task to completion.

There is an old saying that applies to the objective of CBA. It is: "The more you do; the more you can do." We should also add, "Success breeds success." Success and academic learning time go together. Doing and succeeding produce achievement. Doing and succeeding are necessary benefits of curriculum based assessment and instruction. They are necessary if children are to achieve to their potential.

Curing Individual Differences

All too often individual differences in learning ability are viewed as curable maladies. However, our attempts to cure them produce more casualties. We make the misguided attempt to force the children to perform up to grade level standards. A quarter typically and unfortunately fail. The actual range of academic capability in each of the primary grades is at least two and one-half years. By the time primary-age children reach high school, the range exceeds five years; it more than doubles. This widening range should be viewed as being as normal as the expected differences in height, motor-skill development, artistic or musical talent, etc. CBA is intended to provide a means for accepting and working with he range of readiness levels and learning rates that always exist.

Programming for Success

Programming for success in the face of such a great range of individual differences can be intimidating. However, living with the consequences of not programming for the success of children with these differences often is demoralizing. There is nothing more dear to the heart of a teacher than having children on-task and successfully completing their assignments.

Children who are failing and have little work that they can do or complete, demonstrate other behaviors that contribute to the demoralization. The children will be off-task in a variety of ways, some of which are disruptive or annoying. Chronic failure will attack and then erode the child's self-concept. This state produces still more negative behavioral consequences. In fact, much of the negative behavior associated with learning disabled children is attributable to chronic failure and frustration.

Dealing with individual differences effectively is very hard work. However, dealing with the consequences of not doing so is really much harder. CBA is a technique developed to help teachers deal effectively with individual differences.

The learning problems of all LD children are not necessarily simply the result of a mismatch between their ability and curricular demands. There is a small percentage of LD students whose learning problems are caused to greater or lesser extent by central nervous system abnormality. There are also some whose problems are the result of nutritional or metabolic disorders. Social factors contribute in some instances a well. CBA directly addresses these problems, and methods of attending to them will be considered later in the book. Even with these children, however, matching the curriculum to the individual is of primary importance.

Some subsequent chapters further consider the relationship between the structure of the curriculum and the LD or LA child. Some chapters deal with assessment issues and how CBA should influence them. The rest of the book is devoted to the management of individual differences in instructional needs through the use of CBA.

CHAPTER 2

SUCCESS OR CHALLENGE

A Double Standard

WHY IS IT that only low achieving students should be challenged? If students lag behind grade level standards, they are the ones who are challenged. "They'll never learn if they're not challenged," is an often heard expression in regard to low achieving students. However, as Forell (1985) points out so well, the history of higher achieving students has been one of success and of always being comfortable in their instructional materials. On the other hand, low-achievers are frequently challenged with materials above their skill level.

Success is fully evident in the performance of higher-achieving students. In reading groups they read easily and fluently. They encounter few unknown words. Their comprehension is high. In arithmetic and other content areas, the same evidence appears as well. Their performance is marked by comfortable success.

It should be obvious that this level of success is important for achievement. Low achieving students deserve the same standard as the high achieving ones. Low-achievers need a comfortable placement on the curricular path in order to achieve to their potential. Remember; success is fundamental to achievement. Lack of success hampers achievement. The double standard should be eliminated. This criterion of success needs to be use for all students.

Why We Require Failure

If success is so important a factor in achievement, why do we require so much failure? Tradition may be one answer; that's the way we've always done it. Another answer likely is that teachers are misled by the success of the majority of their students. If so many students do so well, certainly the rest of them could if they really tried. Teachers feel a

9

powerful need to have students working at grade level. Using grade level materials gives the appearance of working at grade level, even if the student is failing. That is the way the curriculum is structured and that is the way all of the basal instructional material is structured as well. These are strong factors affecting the expectations we have for students in each chronological age group.

Other reasons have to do with the maintenance of "standards." This notion assumes that some students always fail. After all, isn't that why we have grades? A related argument is that giving lower grades makes it more important to work harder. Students who are doing poorly haven't been challenged enough.

We must break from the practice of requiring failure. Low achieving students are challenged far too much. The double standard must be abandoned. Failure produces no increase in achievement. It is inhumane. We should not compel primary age children to endure continued frustration and failure. There are no benefits.

Why Failure Fails

Failure precludes the conditions necessary for achievement. The harder an instructional activity is for a student, the slower and more painstaking is his progress through it. In reading selections, he will struggle with word identification of many words. Too many new words reduces the effective use of context; comprehension suffers. Finally, when it is too hard, the student cannot maintain his attention on the task. He simply can't do it. He is no longer actively engaged in the activity. Learning time is limited or eliminated entirely. Yet, academic learning time is necessary for achievement. This is true for all instructional areas.

The student is also missing two additional important benefits of appropriately matched instructional materials. These two benefits are success and the reward gained from completing a task. These two benefits are enormously encouraging to a student (Hargis, 1982).

Continued failure produces a wide range of negative behaviors in children. At the daily activity level, tasks that are too difficult cannot maintain a student's attention. Students will very shortly be off-task if they can't do the assignment. The range of off-task behavior will range from quiet day dreaming to annoying disturbances. This requires nonproductive teacher attention.

Continued failure often erodes the self concept and self confidence of children. This can have further compounding behavioral effects.

Learned Helplessness (Grimes, 1981) is a condition where some children lower their expectations of future success and avoid tasks. This condition occurs in some children faced with an imbalance of negative feedback and failure. The less children experience success, the more avoidance behavior they will have. This is a further compounding effect. Children who need more time on task will be learning to avoid the task.

Success

We must learn from our successes and our failures. Success does breed success. Continued failure does foster failure. Children will not willingly or voluntarily fail; failure is imposed.

Success optimizes achievement. We must abandon the notion of achievement to grade level standards. We must aim for achievement to the capacity of each student. This can only be reached by insuring that each child experiences success in the same measure as his higher achieving peer. When this occurs, the curriculum casualty will be eliminated from the list of learning disabilities.

If success is planned, then time on-task can occur. Behavior is modified. Instruction, instead of problem off-task behavior, can then become the focus of the teacher's efforts. The student and teacher enter a positive cycle of success and achievement. The child gains in self-concept and confidence. Children who are increasingly on-task and completing assignments are a joy to any teacher. Real achievement occurs and the quality of instruction appears to be and is better.

Forell (1985) reported a change in her low achieving group from the 23rd percentile to the 48th on the Iowa Tests of Basic Skills after a reading program emphasizing success was implemented. Improvements in scores of the extremes of any population has a rather dramatic effect on the mean scores for the group of which they are a part. It is a wise policy to insure the success of the low achieving group. Not only does it benefit the students, but it makes their teacher look very good.

The Objective of CBA

The primary objective of CBA is the success of students. There are two assessment steps in achieving this end and much of the book will be devoted to their details. The first step is finding a level on the curriculum where the student can succeed. Sometimes this is difficult, but the assessment methods are simple and straight-forward. The second step is incorporating assessment practices in the daily teaching activities so that success is an ongoing affair. Assessment will become the intimate companion of instruction; and, in fact, it should become an intrinsic part of instruction.

Since success becomes the primary objective under CBA, the focus of assessment practice must change to what skills a child has. Success and achievement must be built on what the child can do. Almost any test LD and LA children get will show a multitude of deficits, but it is more important to identify strengths. Finding assessment devices and procedures to locate strength will be given much more consideration later.

CBA must also provide detailed directions on the preparation and identification of appropriate instructional material which produce the success objective. Here, the assessment procedure checks student performance and the adequacy of the instructional activities and materials simultaneously. This dimension of assessment will be considered in some detail later.

Whose Fault?

Often, when a child fails or does poorly in school we assume that the cause is within the child. We begin to look for evidence of a disability. The most trivial behavioral evidence may be used find a label for the child. If this evidence happens to be lacking, the child may simply be labeled as lazy.

When children are blamed, particularly if they are considered slow or lazy, they may have the added pain of punishment. The following incident illustrates such an instance in the case of two fifth-grade boys who were kept in from recess to complete work they had not finished in class: Looking over the uncompleted seatwork, it was apparent that it was considerably too difficult for either boy. Their responses were mostly errors, and they seemed to be mainly random guessing. However, the reaction and attitude of the two boys was contrasting. One boy was innured and somewhat surly. He slouched in his seat and drummed his pencil on the desk top. He was making no attempt to finish his work. He looked disdainfully at his teary-eyed companion who was moving his paper and pencil fitfully over his desk top, hoping, possibly, that a different perspective might miraculously make the work doable. Then the first boy said to the distraught one, "I can sit here till the bus leaves. It doesn't bother me." He had hardened himself to the discomfort of the loss of free time at school. He knew that the school bus would always come to rescue him. I couldn't help feeling admiration for the boy's durability. He had learned to cope with failure. On the other hand, I couldn't help but feel sympathy for the other child. The anxiety affect of failure was quite evident in his manner. Both of these children deserve fairer treatment. How different their circumstances would be if the curriculum had been adjusted to fit them.

If there is blame to be placed, it should be on the lack of assessment procedures that sensitively place children on instructional pathways where failure does not result. When children are permitted to work where they should, they normally succeed, and unfortunate situations like those illustrated above do not occur.

The Same Scores

The notion that all children must succeed by design has a novel effect. If success is planned, it means that all children will demonstrate roughly the same response levels in the work they do. High scores indicate success. The result of a good match between instructional material and student is a high level of performance.

Think of the system as basically the reverse of standard practice. In most classrooms, the students are given the standard instructional material on the same place in the curricular ladder. The children always vary in ability, so we expect some students to do very well and others to do poorly. When curriculum-based assessment is used, the instructional material must be varied to produce similar scores in all the children. Curriculum-based assessment covaries instruction with student skill level. "Standard practice" imposes the same material on variable students, thus producing variable scores.

Scores, when using CBA, should appear in the narrow band that indicates the student is on-task, engaged in learning and succeeding. Only a fairly narrow performance band is acceptable.

Varying instruction, not scores, is fundamental to CBA.

Answering the Skeptics

Certain comments and questions arise when these notions are presented. "How can a classroom teacher, with 25 to 30 students, manage this?" "It sounds good, but it would cost too much money."

The answer to these questions is that teachers have provided and continue to provide, students functioning at several different grade levels in one classroom with appropriately differentiated instruction.

Literally tens of thousands of children are taught in small rural schools where a single teacher frequently serves more than one grade level at once. One still finds classrooms that are made up of all the primary grades or the intermediate grades or the middle school grades. There are many high schools with graduating classes of under a dozen. Here, teachers routinely manage many levels and subjects, and, I should add they often do it quite well.

Dealing with many different levels of instruction in one room is simply a matter of your expectation. In multigraded classrooms, one expects to deal with quite different levels of instruction, so it is done. In single-grade classrooms, we think we have reduced the student variation, but we haven't. The actual instructional levels of the students always cover several years. Teachers should expect to provide instruction at these different levels. It requires different organizational practices, but a great many teachers already manage to do this as if it were commonplace routine.

As to the comment concerning money, the cost should be no different than for the operation of any other classroom with the same number of students in that school system. The curricular materials that are already available will need redistribution so that a variety of levels will be available in each classroom, but no new material is needed.

Remember; teachers deal with the differences in their classroom one-way-or-the-other, like-it-or-not. It seems it would be far better for teachers to deal with problems of variable instruction than to deal with the problems of achievement and behavior.

CHAPTER 3

ASSESSMENT THAT IS CURRICULUM BASED

IN CBA, assessment is used for preventing failure and programming success. To do this, it must provide direct guidance in planning daily instructional activities. As its name shows, assessment must be drawn from the curriculum that is the basis for instruction. All too often tests exist quite independently from the curriculum being used. They are used to classify children or to classify their problems. They are of no direct help in meeting the daily curricular/instructional demands placed on teachers and students. The November, 1985 issue of the journal *Exceptional Children* was devoted to curriculum-based assessment, and it covers this problem of test relevance in detail. Tests that are not curriculum based often are wasted effort, and the worst have negative effects. Tests that have relevance to teachers and students speak to the substantive demands of daily instruction and materials preparation, and thus are curriculum based.

Some Assessment Terms

Validity is the most important quality of any test. A valid test measures exactly what you want to measure and nothing else. An important type of validity is content validity. Tests should relate with precision to what is being taught. Tests that do this have content validity. Content validity is the required form of validity for most curriculum-based assessment. In order for a test to have content validity, the test should be made up of a sufficient number of items from the curricular area being measured. A test with an adequate representation of such items can accurately measure the level of achievement in that particular area.

The validity of some tests is determined by comparing it with established instruments that are used to measure the same things. This

15

type of validity is called criterion-related validity. This form of validity assumes that the established instrument is itself valid. At any rate, this form of validity in no way assures that the test has a sufficient representation of items concerning the area being measured to give it content validity. Many standard diagnostic and achievement tests bear more resemblance to other tests than they do to the content of the curriculum being measured. Research by Jenkins and Pany (1978) shows that most standardized reading tests did not representatively sample the content of different reading curricula. Significant biases appear to exist which in turn suggest that student achievement in a particular curriculum may not be reflected in achievement test scores.

The content from reading curriculum to another varies substantially. This is also true of mathematics curricula, social studies, science, etc. It is highly unlikely that standardized tests could accurately assess progress or placement on any given curriculum. For maximum validity, teachers should have curriculum-based tests — tests that adequately sample skills presented on the curriculum in actual use. Mastery and progress toward mastery of curricular objectives is what needs to be measured. Tests that are specific to particular curricula are necessary to do this.

Predictive validity is the extent to which a test predicts later success in a skill area of concern. Predictive validity is an important consideration when selecting readiness tests. Readiness tests are necessary to head off failure. Readiness tests need sufficient predictive accuracy to identify children who are at risk for failure. Intervention at the readiness level is far more productive than pushing a student into instructional activities that are too difficult.

High predictive validity is difficult to achieve. After all, a skill not yet attained does not readily provide items for a test. Remember, content validity is achieved by making sure that components of the skill comprise the test. However, on readiness tests, items that seem to be subskills of the criterion skill are about all that can be used. Readiness tests, especially reading-readiness tests, cannot predict all levels of later reading achievement with accuracy. However, they can do one very important job of prediction quite well; readiness tests do identify children who will have trouble in learning to read. Here rests the importance of readiness tests and predictive validity. Readiness tests with sufficient predictive validity to predict likelihood of failure need to be adopted. More important than their adoption and use, the information obtained from them needs to be acted upon.

Reliability is a characteristic of valid tests. Reliable tests are dependable; they give consistent results. Reliable tests are made up of well constructed, unambiguous items. Reliability and validity are occasionally confused because the coefficients used for both are the same (from 0.00 to 1.00), there is a necessary relationship between the two. Reliability is a necessary characteristic of a valid test, but a test that gives consistent results does not necessarily measure the thing you want it to. Reliability is primarily impotant because it is necessary for validity.

Reliability becomes an important consideration for teachers constructing informal or curriculum-referenced tests for classroom use. These are the most-used tests in teaching. In the formulation of tests, unless care is taken to reduce error caused by ambiguous or confusing test items, inaccurate assessment information will result.

Types of Tests

Norm-referenced tests constitute the bulk of published tests. Norm-referenced means that they have been given to groups representing certain populations. These may be populations assembled by age, sex, grade level, geographic area, etc. With these tests, depending on the normative information furnished, an individual can be compared with the norms, or a group's performance can be compared with normative group performance.

I have been stressing the use of curriculum-based tests. However, norm-referenced tests may be used in a variety of beneficial ways. Reading-readiness tests are typically norm-referenced. Norm-referenced tests can be used in program evaluation or for accountability. However, they usually are not helpful in determining specific instructional objectives, unless the items on the test correspond very closely to those that make up the curriculum. Usually these tests can sample only a few items from any level of a curriculum and so can only have limited instructional use.

In recent years, **criterion-referenced** tests have attracted some interest. Criterion-referenced tests were supposed to differ from norm-referenced tests in that they were designed to evaluate an individual's level of performance or mastery of some specific instructional objectives. Actually curriculum-based assessment does this. The word "curriculum" was specifically selected to indicate that the instructional objectives to be measured must be those taken from the curriculum which is guiding instruction. Also, many so-called criterion referenced tests are published for general use and are no more likely to represent a specific curriculum criterion than are norm referenced tests. In recent years, we have seen the development of criterion-referenced tests with norms and norm-referenced tests that have criterion-referenced interpretations. Obviously, the distinction between the two has markedly diminished.

Screening tests should be used to avoid placing children in failure situations. Also, they should be used to discover which children are making less progress in reading than they might potentially achieve. Vision, hearing and readiness tests should be routinely administered for these reasons. These tests may be used to refer children for further evaluation. Screening tests may lack precision. However, inaccuracy in the direction of over-referral from such tests is preferable to under-referral.

Diagnostic tests usually refer to assessment procedures that are used to identify the specific needs of students with learning problems. Often in the past, they have been associated with the identification of the cause of the problem, the classification of the handicapping condition or the labeling of children. More current notions of diagnostic assessment makes it a guide to the instructional process. This is often called diagnostic-prescriptive teaching or more simply just prescriptive teaching. In this approach to teaching, assessment is carefully articulated with the provided instruction. This is precisely the intent of curriculum-based assessment. However, so-called diagnostic tests seldom accurately sample skill deficiency specific to any one particular curriculum. In fact, if one chooses to use some diagnostic test then one is obliged to teach to the revealed deficiencies as though the test were the curriculum. This phenomenon causes a set of difficulties that frequently confound the problem of the instruction of LA and LD students—but more will be said about this later.

Proponents of diagnostic tests and of prescriptive teaching claim that strengths and weaknesses are assessed. However, the focus of diagnosis and the subsequent intervention typically emphasize weakness or skill deficiency. There are no stated formulas or systematic approaches to balancing the measurement of weaknesses and strength and then programming them equally through the prescription.

The term "diagnosis," whether in medicine or education, implies the identification of a problem. However, it is critically important to identify what a child knows or what skills he has. Knowledge of strength is necessary to prepare instructional materials and activities that produce success and academic learning time. From hard experience, the author has found what happens when one falls into the diagnostic trap of identifying deficiencies. A variety of activities are planned to remediate these deficiencies; then it is found that these activities are frustrating and non-productive for the student. This unfortunate situation occurs because the work is made up entirely of items that the student doesn't know — the assumed deficiencies. The student is systematically, if unwittingly, over-whelmed with work that is too difficult.

With CBA, diagnostic information focuses on strength more than weakness. Success is produced by appropriately balancing knowns with unknowns in all instructional activities. Strengths must predominate. Much more will be said about this important feature of CBA later.

A **case history** can provide insight into a student's learning problem through knowledge of his background and development.

Some information will have immediate relevance to the remedial action taken in the classroom. How much a child has had to eat or how much sleep he gets will affect his behavior at school. What language is spoken at home can influence curricular needs. The child's health both physical and emotional will affect his school performance.

Information concerning a child's past and present status in family and community are important. Health and nutritional information are equally important. Children with empty stomachs are more likely to benefit from a peanut butter sandwich than from a curricular adjustment.

Avoiding Failure

The time to prevent failure in school is before formal instruction starts. We are in a rush to start instruction and when it is begun, we make every effort to force children to achieve at grade level. The inevitable result of this practice is failure in far too large a percentage of children.

Readiness assessment is important. More important is that information that suggests lack of readiness be acted on. If children are not ready to start first grade, there are several options that should be available on their behalf. These options include a delay of starting first grade, compensatory readiness programming or an extension of the readiness period from a few months to even a year or two.

Readiness tests have often been criticized for being imprecise measures. For example, the predictive validity of popular reading-readiness tests ranges from about .50 to .70. These coefficients are obtained by correlating these tests scores with level of reading achievement at the end of the first grade. Such coefficients do not permit accurate prediction of reading achievement for individual students. However, these tests do perform remarkably well in predicting which children will fail. The most important use of readiness tests is to locate kindergarten age children who are likely to fail and not to predict specific achievement levels.

Standardized reading-readiness tests accurately identify about 80 percent of the children who are not ready. However, when using instruments, the results should be moderated by teacher judgement. Obviously, some children will fail who are not identified by readiness tests. They will fail because of factors not sampled by the tests. For these children, teacher judgement and the information gained from case histories will be the only means of identifying potential failure.

Assessment for Teaching

Curriculum-referenced tests should be used to identify a child's current level of functioning within the curricula in use. A starting place or a readiness level is most accurately established with curriculum-referenced tests. Curriculum-referenced tests are made up of curriculum items. Only with this degree of specificity can validity be insured. The level a child can reasonably be expected to achieve on a particular curriculum can only be found by determining his comfortable instructional level on a test that adequately samples items from that curriculum. Some reading and mathematics curricula provide progress or placement tests that can be used to measure some of their components, but accurate placement is determined by the evaluation of the students performance on various levels of activities or reading selections sampled from those that will be a part of daily instruction. The level being sought is called the instructional level. This level was first defined by Emmett Betts (1946) in regard to reading difficulty levels. The nature and details of instructional levels will be covered in the next chapter, but briefly, for reading, it is the level of difficulty where a student encounters no more than four percent new words and has a comprehension level of at least 75 percent. This is the maximum level of difficulty where a student can remain on-task without symptoms of tension and frustration.

Besides the assessment to determine readiness, entry level or instructional level, there must routine direct evaluation based on instruction and materials in daily use. In CBA, evaluation is a central component of instruction itself. It is fundamentally checking the instructional match between activity of material and the student it is being used with. This is not as great a chore as it may sound. Already, seat work, worksheets and homework are routinely checked. We routinely listen to children reading orally. We use this information to give grades on daily work. Essentially the same procedure is followed with the routine of curriculum-based assessment, but instead of assigning a grade to the student, the information is used to see if an instructional match has been made. For example, if the student has missed too many items on the math worksheet that will suggest that there are too many new or hard items for him to manage. The material might require further examination to see if the student has the prerequisite skills necessary to do the items that were missed. When listening to a child's oral reading, the number of words he stumbles over or can't identify should not suggest a letter grade but the appropriateness for that child. In effect, we should grade the material or activity not the child.

If the child does not or cannot complete assigned work, the difficulty level of the work should be reviewed. If a child is frequently off-task or shows signs of tension and frustration when he is, the difficulty level of the work should be studied. The very processes of instruction are assessment information when it is curriculum based.

Acting on information gained in this way means that the curriculum level must be gauged individually. An individual's maximum progress will only occur if he is given work that he can stay on-task with and complete with comprehension. These are simply the conditions that exist for virtually all students who are making adequate or better progress in school, and we should expect no less for our slow and disabled learners. These are conditions that produce success and progress. In order to achieve these conditions for students who have low achievement and learning disabilities, assessment must be an intimate part of daily instruction. All instruction should be viewed as a form of assessment. But remember; this will be more assessment of instruction and material than of student. It is necessary to observe and record the students performance, but the grade is reserved for the instructional activity itself.

Test Relevance

Choose your tests well for they will likely become your curriculum. Witness the coming of the "proficiency" test throughout the country. Teachers nationwide devote increasing time teaching to it. It is important that their students pass the proficiency test. I have no argument whatever with teaching to a test; that is essentially what curriculum-based assessment is about. If the objectives measured on the proficiency test are important, then they should be taught. The proficiency test is then dictating the contents of the curriculum. I would even hope that the regular curriculum would be compatible with the contents of the proficiency test. If they are not compatible, then the curriculum probably should be abandoned for one that is, or the proficiency test should simply be adopted as a part of the curriculum.

"Teaching the test" should not be such a pejorative expression. You should be testing what you teach and teaching what you test. Remember the discussion of "content validity." A test must be comprised of a sufficient number of items from the topic under consideration in order to have content validity. Content validity is attained by using the curriculum as the bases for assessment. Another way of attaining it is to make the test the basis of the curriculum. This will be well and good if the test contains the range of appropriate and desirable items that should be in a curriculum.

Often teachers or psychologist administer various tests to children with learning difficulties. A wide variety of such tests are routinely given. The tests themselves may have no relevance to the child's curriculum. However, deficiencies in skills, perception or assorted aptitudes are invariably found. Often the deficiency has nothing to do with what is going on in instruction. Yet, the identification of the deficiency prompts the development of an ancillary remedial curriculum to deal with this supposed deficit. Sometimes these new curricula replace or parallel the existing program. Often this new intervention, which was based on noncurriculum-referenced tests, only fragments or dilutes the time spent on regular curricular activities. Children who need more time actively engaged in reading or math activities on their regular curriculum are getting less. These new tests have dictated new curricula. Remember, choose your tests well for they may become your curriculum.

Many standardized tests are intended to measure word-identification subskills. Tests of such subskills are unlikely to have content validity when they are compared with specific reading curricula. A tremendous variety of reading subskills forms a large part of virtually all reading programs. These word-identification subskills are presented in different sequences with different emphasis from one to the next. Items considered important in one may be overlooked in the next. Published tests cannot sample the scope and sequence of subskills presented in a given reading curriculum unless they are prepared for that curriculum. When noncurriculum-based tests are administered to children with reading problems, they will very likely show subskill deficiencies measured by those tests. However, they may not be the ones that have been or are being presented in the curriculum to those children. The danger with using such tests is that the evidence of deficiency may produce a program to remediate it. A new curriculum based on invalid evidence may be started. The new curriculum displaces time that might be used with the regular curriculum. Achievement is not enhanced.

Reading curricula are often designed to fit test results. This is a basic tenet of prescriptive teaching. A subskill deficiency on some diagnostic test does not necessarily mean that more and more emphasis should be placed on teaching that subskill. Do not let supposed subskills dominate either assessment or the reading curriculum. The author has witnessed situations where students receive whole remedial programs based on subskill deficits, few of which are common to the regular curriculum. Teachers vest tremendous credibility in published tests. A poor reader did poorly on these tests; therefore, deficiencies revealed by them must be remediated. The cause of the reading problem is the deficits revealed by these tests. Validity is almost never considered. The students who are the recipients of this practice are not beneficiaries. The bulk of reading instruction centers on learning subskills that have been carefully identified as missing; adequate success is not considered, and worst of all; time that could have been spent at really reading is virtually eliminated.

Measures of actual reading from the reading material that is available in the curriculum are the most important gauge of reading progress and the best guides to formulating specific instructional activities. Two types of informal assessment are most useful. One is word-recognition assessment (the difference between word-recognition and word-identification will be considered in a later chapter). These tests should be based on the words being introduced in a student's reading program. The other is the assessment of silent and oral reading of specific selections from the student's reading material. These two types of tests should be used to determine the placement, to check achievement after teaching and to evaluate and prepare reading materials for specific children.

Teaching and Testing

The use of instructional material that is too difficult results in failure and with failure goes its attendant behaviors. On the other hand, these same behaviors can be the cause rather than the result of failure. In this case, the focus of instruction must include an emphasis on the control of the interfering behavior. If the difficulty of the material is the cause of a student's off-task behavior, then it is a matter of adjusting the instructional materials. However, this will also be necessary even if the behaviors themselves are contributing to the learning problems. One cannot simply focus on behavior without attending to the difficulty of the activity being taught.

The first stage of assessment is to find out how much ability the student has and then prepare or identify the activity or material that will fit within that skill level. This material should maintain attention and be completed with comprehension. This is the instructional level. The instructional level will be a subject of the next chapter.

After the instructional level has been identified, the second stage of assessment can occur. This is observation of students working at an appropriate level of difficulty. The off-task behaviors that remain after sufficient opportunity to get used to working at this level are then the focus of assessment. The persisting off-task behaviors may likely be the cause of a learning problem and can require an intervention that gives specific attention to modifying them. In other words, when a child remains inattentive or distracted from instructional activities that are clearly within his ability, the attention problem, the distractability or any other off-task behaviors will need dealing with. However, ample time must be provided to observe the child working at carefully prepared instructional level activities. Children who have experienced nothing but failure and frustration in school, often for years, will have developed a set attitude and behavior pattern when facing any instructional activity. However, finding success in an activity that usually produces discomfort is so immediately rewarding that most students are very shortly on-task.

The best form of intervention is most accurately determined by the observation of residual behaviors as was outlined above. It is only in this way that a teacher can be certain of whether off-task behavior is a cause or a symptom and which must be dealt with.

Much of the data for identifying or preparing instructional material must come from the continued observation and testing that occurs during teaching. The preparation of instructional material will be necessary as long as the student's instructional level and need for repetition and practice lie outside that provided by the available published material. For example, through teaching and testing a teacher will determine the amount of repetition of a word a child needs to learn it. In basal reading problems, there is inconsistent, often spotty repetition of words once they have been introduced. This is a major problem for the low achieving student. The teacher will of necessity provide the required additional repetition for these words in supplementary activities if the student is to get any benefit from the basal reader at all.

Finding Problems

Unfortunately, it most often takes a student's failure to confirm the existence of a problem. Failure should not be our primary identification instrument. Children should never be required to fail before appropriate instructional steps are taken. Failure occurs in two ways, one obvious the other not. Failure is obvious when a child falls behind the ongoing level of instruction. This inability to work at grade level stands out, and it is frequently accompanied by other distracting behaviors. The less obvious failure occurs when a student has a potential for achievement that is higher than his grade level of placement but is functioning well only at that placement level. There will be no failure related behavior because the instructional demands do not exceed the child's ability. For this reason, the problem is quite likely to go unnoticed. Some would not call this failure, but it certainly is failure to achieve to potential.

Among those who cannot perform at grade-level standards, there is a common cause. That cause is their failing work. Failure is not productive, so the more a child fails the further he falls behind his potential.

A problem exists if a student is not achieving to the level of his capacity or potential indicates. Therefore, a measure of potential is required to determine the existence of such a problem or discrepancy.

The most relevant measures of reading potential are listening comprehension tests. If selections are taken from each of the grade levels of reading materials being used by a particular student, then the test will be curriculum-based.

The procedure for preparing a listening comprehension test is the same as for preparing an informal reading inventory. However, instead of the student reading the test to find his instructional reading level, the teacher reads the test aloud to the student to find the highest level where the student attains at least 70 percent comprehension. This is the student's listening comprehension level. It indicates the level of reasonable achievement potential for the student. You can learn to read language that is unfamiliar **only** in print.

This informal approach to determining reading capacity level is curriculum-based. It is directly related to the reading materials that are to be used. Thus, the relevance and validity of the measurement is insured.

There is one good standardized reading capacity test. It is the Diagnostic Reading Scales. Each of the graded passages is matched with considerable precision to the readability level of each grade. The reliability of the comprehension questions has been established. If there is a discrepancy, it can be determined by using the test for establishing both the instructional reading level and the listening comprehension level of a student in the same way as it is with the teacher-made, curriculum-based that was described above. However, especially at the primary grade levels. *The Diagnostic Reading Scales* may lack the relevance and precision that curriculum-based tests have.

Intelligence tests are used to determine capacity or potential. Intelligence tests have fairly high correlations with academic achievement. They are typically required in the identification of learning disabled children. Here, a discrepancy between achievement and the potential established by the score on an "intelligence" test is used to verify the existence of a learning disability. This degree of precision may be sufficient for administrative purposes, but for the teacher, the more accurate and relevant curriculum-based procedures are necessary in instruction.

Changes in Assessment

Assessment that serves the instructional needs of students is curriculum-based. Fitting the curriculum to a student to produce success and reasonable, attainable levels of achievement requires new directions and new objectives for assessment. These differences have been the subject of this chapter. No new techniques or tests have been revealed. The techniques and tests are standard, even mundane. How they relate to instruction, however, is quite different than standard practice.

One difference is the notion of curriculum-basing; this seems to legitimize "teaching the test." In fact, CBA has been called the ultimate in teaching the test (Tucker, 1985). This is all true but in the best sense. Curriculum basing insures test validity and the relevance of the instruction that results from such measurement.

Another difference is that assessment's main function is to insure success in instructional activities. Therefore, assessment information is used to prepare appropriate instructional level activities and materials for each student.

Insuring success requires a different focus of assessment. If success is the focus of assessment, the data of evaluation is used to grade the materials or the activities appropriateness of fit to the student. The instructional activity or material is graded moreso than the student. Further, attending to success means that instruction must be used as assessment. The normal grading or scoring of seatwork, homework, drill, etc. takes on an institutionalized status. It is the regular ongoing fundamental form of the bulk of curriculum-based assessment. However, it is not for the purpose of giving the student a grade; it is to make certain there is an instructional match between curriculum level and student.

Another difference is the shift in focus from weaknesses to strengths of a student. Children who have made painfully small amounts of progress have few, often well concealed strengths. Primary attention must be given to finding them. Success must be built on strengths and skills. In instructional level reading known words out number unknowns at least ninety-five to five. Attention maintaining drill and seatwork in math require that only about a quarter of the items can be new and unfamiliar. The rest must be more familiar items that are being reviewed and practiced. In all instances the ratio of knowns and dominate. They are the helpful context in reading that support the identification of the new and unknown words. They may provide helpful contextual support in math drill work. Finally, the high proportion of knowns permits students to feel the high reinforcement of success and accomplishment that is routine for their higher achieving peers.

Another difference is the observation of off-task behavior. Off-task behavior results from a poor instructional match. However, if there is persisting off-task behavior after a good match is made, then an additional curricular emphasis dealing with the behaviors may be appropriate.

Standardized testing is not emphasized in CBA, but it is used. It has two primary functions. One is in preventing failure. The use of readiness tests is an important function here. Accountability and program evaluation is another appropriate use. Norm-referenced measures here can provide information on how well the teacher or program is performing, given similar students and circumstances.

A novel difference exists between curriculum based assessment and most other form of assessment. If norm-referenced tests are given to the students in any classroom, a great variation in scores on the tests would be expected. We expect this wide variation scores on any test administered to the group whether teacher-made or standardized. However, with curriculum-based assessment, one is trying to achieve approximately the same scores from all the students. The curriculum itself is used to form the test, and if the level of the curriculum is adjusted appropriately to fit the individual students instructional needs, then the scores should reflect that these needs have been met. In other words, curricular materials vary in difficulty; scores stay about at the same level which indicates that the students are meeting with success. This is a major change from standard practice where test scores must vary because curriculum materials and activities are kept at a relatively uniform level. CBA is a tuning process where level of instruction is continually matched with student skill. Instructional delivery is tuned to the student by making sure that performance in the instructional material stays within the prescribed limits. Really, the tests themselves vary because they are comprised of the actual instructional material being used with individual students.

Instruction and assessment are fused in this system. How assessment is integrated in instructional activities and how assessment is used to prepare instructional activities and materials are the subjects of subsequent chapters.

CHAPTER 4

INSTRUCTIONAL LEVELS AND RATES
IN READING

THE MATCH between a student and the curriculum needs to be made very specifically. This match must be made at the specific level of instructional activity in material that is used to achieve curricular goals. It is at this daily level of activity where the student must meet with instruction that produces the success, comprehension, on-task behavior and learning time that is needed to achieve. The subject of this chapter is the nature of instructional activity and material that must be provided in this match. CBA is the matching process; instructional levels and rates are the criterion indexes of the accuracy of the match.

Assessment is used to make the match initially, and it is used throughout instruction to maintain it. Instructional activities and materials do not have some built in or fixed level of difficulty. The level of difficulty is relative to individual students. For example, the designation of a grade level of difficulty for some basal reading material is at best only a normative index. In other words, the material is appropriate for the "average" student in this age range. Actually, however, the only way that the difficulty level of any instructional material can be determined for a specific child is by letting that child use it to see how hard it actually is. Fundamentally, this is what curriculum based assessment does, and it is done as a part of all instructional activity.

The instructional level of any material exists only in regard to the individuals who use it. It can be said that there is a normative level and an instructional level for instructional material. A normative level is the level usually stated by the publisher. It can be determined by a readability formula or by testing it with groups of children. Sometimes even more subjective methods are used to determine difficulty level, but whatever the method, at best, it can only approximate the difficulty level for groups of students, not individuals. The instructional level is determined by measuring a student's performance in that particular material.

The nature of a student's performance on some specific material determines its instructional level for that student. The nature of this performance can be quantified, and this quantified performance can be compared to objective performance standards that indicate the instructional level. If there is a gap between the student's performance and the standards then different materials need to be obtained or the materials need to be modified so that the match can be made.

Teaching as Testing

Teachers must view what they are teaching as a test. The student's performance is the test's results. There are important results to be noted on the student's performance in each teaching activity: The number of words a student does not know and his fluency when reading orally; his response to questions that indicate the comprehension level of a selection just read; the percent correct on a phonics worksheet or a drill activity in math. This is just to mention a few of the activities that produce measurable responses; virtually all of teaching does just this. These responses form the basis for judgements about the difficulty level of a specific material or activity for a specific student. Making the match between student and instruction only requires a little more systematic observation of performance during daily activities.

Usually when performance on daily activity is noted, it is for the purpose of assigning grades. However, it should be for the purpose of identifying, adjusting or maintaining the appropriate instructional level of instruction for the students. Poor performance is indicative of a poor match between student and instructional material. When students are constantly performing poorly in school, primary test evidence is being ignored.

Observation of performance on daily activities can provide the essential information on how to make an accurate match between student and instructional level and instructional rate. The subject of this chapter is the characteristics of instructional level activities and materials.

Instructional Level in Reading

Gates (1930) first addressed the problem of vocabulary burden in beginning reading instruction. When Gates began studying the problem of vocabulary burden in the 1920's, the available primary reading material introduced new words in the range of 1 in 10 to 1 in 17 running words. This range had been far too difficult and teachers routinely had to provide much supplementary teacher-made material to enable their students to read these books at all. He found that one new word in 60 was a manageable introduction rate for most beginning readers. Gates's research had a marked, beneficial impact on word introduction rates in basal readers. Beginning in the 1930's, basal readers generally conformed to his guidelines for word introduction. His reseach made beginning reading materials accessible to the majority of students.

Controlling the introduction of words in reading instructional materials was an important step, but simply controlling the introduction of words does not mean that the new vocabulary load will remain the same for all students. A word may remain unfamiliar for a long time after too many new ones have been introduced. Emmett Betts (1946) studied the problem of how many strange words a student can manage in a reading activity before his comprehension breaks down, and he shows signs of frustration. His research produced the definition of the "instructional reading level." He also described the level of difficulty to be avoided. He called it the "frustration level." In general, the instructional level occurs when a student encounters new or unknown words in the range of 2 to 4 percent. With a vocabulary load of this size, a student usually can attain a 75 percent comprehension level, if he is receiving some teaching assistance.

Betts also described another important reading level. He called it the "basal level" or the "recreational level." It is sometimes called the "independent level," because at this level, the student can read independently with no teaching assistance. At the independent level, a student will encounter fewer than two percent unknown words, and his comprehension level will be at least 90 percent.

The instructional level is important because it gives the maximum leeway for introducing new words, while permitting comprehension and attention maintenance. The independent reading level is important in that it is the level that indicates mastery. It is the level where a child can read recreationally and learn to enjoy reading. It is the level where a student can attain fluency and expand his instant, word recognition vocabulary. All students need curricular time devoted to these two levels.

The frustration level is nonproductive and is to be avoided. When a student encounters more than about four percent unknown words, signs of stress appear and comprehension usually breaks down rapidly.

Children given frustration level work will demonstrate little on-task be-havior in silent reading, and their oral reading will show clear evidence of the number of words unknown to them.

In order to remind the mature reader of what it is like to cope with the number of unknown words that beginning readers encounter, sev-eral selections have been prepared. These selections use obscure or con-trived words to insure that the same impact is made. The first selection has about 7 percent unknown words:

> The man leaned against the current as he waded, waist-deep, up-stream. His hands steadied either end of the furnwunch balanced across his shoulders. He had moved about 90 yards from the denup where he had entered the stream. A few yards ahead, a part of the wooded bank had been replaced by a acnrid frud. He came abreast of it, and with effort, pressed the furnwunch up and over his head, and then set it on top of the frud. He placed his hands on his hips, pulled his elbows back and arched his back in an attempt to stretch out muscles that were knotted from the prolonged exertion.
>
> He relaxed somewhat and began a visual inspection of the frud. He moved closer to it and reached under the water to explore its surface. Moving slowly, he started the search from the downstream end. At about the rondtip he stopped and probed one area intently. Satisfied that he had located a grundle he continued to the upstream end. There was only one grundle to contend with. He retrieved the furnwunch and cradled the heavy implement as he made his way back to the rodtip. He gingerly lowered the furnwunch, holding it perpendicular to the frud. When it reached the grundle, he slid it in its full length. He held it in place with one hand and turned the expansion lock handle until the in-strument was seated tightly in place. His mission accomplished, he was clearly relieved. He waded easily downstream to the dnup.

The passage is about 250 words in length. It contains only six unknown words. However, the words are repeated so that there are a total of six-teen occurrences. This amounts to about seven percent unknown words in the passage. The passage would have seemed far more difficult if all of these occurrences had been of different words. Each time a new word is repeated in a context of known words, it attracts additional semantic substance. This passage, however, had too many unknowns to provide the kind of supportive context that is needed to figure out what an un-known word is. Consequently, comprehension of the passage will be ex-tremely limited.

If the number of different unknown words is limited, a passage like the one above can be within the instructional level. This will be true only if there is aprovision for introducing the unknown words before the passage is read, or providing some means for identifying them during the reading activity. If each new word in the passage is counted only once, then the number of unknowns amounts to less than three percent, which is within the instructional range.

The following selection is at the frustration level in any case:

> Long raidans were forming when Mathew arrived. He tried to phindate the amount of time it would take to get to the convorster. Vort it would be too long, plast he would miss the game. He vraxated for a moment until the raidans became even longer. He decided that he would ordrul in the raidan opet see vort it would start moving more expeditiously. No sooner had he started fleedjuul, when it began opet mostulalag quite hard. Mathew became disgusted, zipped up his ornaforger, and walked back to his car. He drove home ov the mostul. By the time he put the car in the garage, the mostul was droim, and the faedos was out. Mathew was doubly disgusted now. Sullenly, he went inside to watch the game. He turned on the television set but nothing happened. Mathew said to himself, "What a lousy frol."

In this passage, thirteen new words are introduced or about nine percent of the total words. The percentage may sound small but the effect on intelligibility is large.

If a student is required to read a passage of similar difficulty orally, the symptoms of frustration level reading would be readily apparent. The refusals and mispronunciations of the unknown words would be the most obvious symptom. The reading would be halting at best, with many slow-downs and stoppages at the new words. Answers to questions directed to the student about the content and meaning of the story would be, at best, guessed at. This is pretty much the behavior the reader would demonstrate if required to read the above passage and then someone privy to the meaning of all the words in the passage asked the comprehension questions.

The next passage is prepared at the independent reading level. Less than two percent of the words are unknown.

> Nathan heard the rubbing sound again. He pulled himself further into the sleeping bag and closed it over his head. There was the sound again! This time the whole tent shook a little. Nathan wished that he had the flashlight with him in the sleeping bag. He was sure a orgillon was trying to get in the tent. Jeff had said that a orgillon would go away if you shone a light on it. Nathan tried to be completely quiet, hoping that the orgillon would think no one was in the tent. It didn't work. The

rubbing and shaking became louder. With all the courage Nathan could muster, he slipped an arm out of the sleeping bag and felt around for the flashlight. He found it and not a pezot too soon. He felt something standing on the sleeping bag. He switched the light on and there, to his surprise and relief, was Gruffy, the pet goat.

The abundance of familiar context helps dealing with the unknown words in this passage. The appearance of unknown words is disconcerting, but context here has sufficient strength to supply much of the necessary meaning to maintain a high level of comprehension.

An important difference exists between the levels of difficulty illustrated above and difficulty levels children actually encounter. This difference is that the unknown words in the children's material should be unfamiliar only in print. This is also a fundamentally important readiness requirement for beginning reading; all of the words should be familiar if spoken or read to the children. In other words, the spoken counterpart of the words are familiar. In this case, familiar context with other word identification skills should assist the student in calling to mind the familiar spoken counterpart of words that are unfamiliar only in print. So, rather than only speculating on the meaning of the unknown words, the student should be able to identify the unknown words without undue effort. Without the support of much known context, the effort required to identify the unknown words is too great and is frustrating. With so much attention necessary in the identification of unknown words, the thread of comprehension will be lost or ignored.

An important attribute of the instructional and independent reading levels, is that they permit and foster time engaged in reading. Research on academically engaged time or academic learning time, shows the direct relationship between the amount of time spent on reading and achievement (Gickling and Thompson, 1985; Rosenshine and Berliner, 1978).

Much has been said about interest and motivation concerning reading materials. However, there is no substitute for supplying students with appropriate instructional level materials. Frustration level materials are neither interesting nor motivating.

Repetition Rates in Reading

How long does it take to learn a word? Far too little attention has been given to this question. Yet, we know that LA and LD students are deficient in the number of "sight words" they know or in the size of their "word recognition" vocabulary. They just don't know enough words to use their basal readers. Gates did the primary work in answering this question many years ago. This important but neglected work suggests the basic guidelines for providing repetition. He studied the repetition requirements of children by levels of intelligence. Table 1 shows Gates's suggested guidelines for word repetition in connected discourse.

TABLE 1

Mean Number of Word Repetitions
Required by IQ Levels

Repetitions	IQ
20	120-129
30	110-119
35	90-109
40	80-89
45	70-79
55	60-69

Adapted from Gates (1930).

Gates emphasized that these numbers were averages and that there was considerable individual variation in the repetition requirements for various words.

Some words are more difficult to learn than others. The characteristic that dominates the learnability of words is imagery level. Imagery level or concreteness of words has to do with how easily a mental image is formed of the referent each word represents. Concrete nouns will have the highest imagery level. They are words like cat, dog, chair, tree, car, bird, etc. Low imagery nouns are words like idea, time, mile, error, belief, etc. High imagery greatly facilitates the learning of words.

Other parts of speech have imagery levels as well. Verbs, adjectives and adverbs can have various levels of imagery; however, the mental image is not distinct from the things they modify or operate with. Even though concrete, the verb run, requires a concrete, animate noun as its subject. Adjectives also require a noun, and adverbs may require an entire sentence. Imagery level remains, however, an important factor in their ease of learning.

Other quite common words, called functions words, have very low imagery levels. These words are articles, auxiliary verbs, relative pronouns, subordinating conjunctions, coordinating conjunctions, etc. It is simply not possible to form a mental image of words like been, are, that, which, at, some, etc. Teachers through the ages have noted the difficulty that some of these most common words have caused beginning readers.

Several research projects have been conducted to determine the differences in difficulty of learning to recognize these various kinds of words by their imagery level (Hargis and Gickling, 1978; Gickling, Hargis and Radford, 1981; Hargis, 1978). Findings here point out that high imagery significantly enhances the development of word recognition, if the words are presented in isolation (the words were presented on flash cards).

Subsequent research has demonstrated the facilitating effect of context on the lower imagery words. In this research, the words were placed in sentences within stories based on experiences. Each of the experimental words were placed in the context of sentences madeup of familiar words. This kind of context had a greatly facilitating effect on lower imagery words. Meaningful, familiar context makes low imagery words as learnable as high imagery words. The study was conducted with a group of LA and LD students. The low imagery words required an average of 58 repetitions in isolation and 47 repetitions in context. There was no significant difference for high imagery nouns. They required about the same repetition in context or isolation.

Notice, though, the amount of repetition required to learn to recognize a word. This need for repetition is unremittent. If these children are to learn to read words, the words require a great deal of repetition. It is preferable that the repetition be provided in meaningful contextual settings whenever possible.

The Dolch Basic Sight Word List (1941) is made up of words most associated with word recognition teaching. These words are often called service words or sight words. They are the most common of all words. These 220 words represent over half of the words used in primary basal readers (Mangieri, 1977). The majority of the words are function words; there are no high imagery nouns on the list.

The commonness and familiarity of these words belie their difficulty. They are the most difficult words for a beginning reader to learn in isolation. When LA and LD children demonstrate problems in learning to read, extra assistance will be provided to them in learning these words. Often their problems are attributed to their limited skill in identifying sight words. Unfortunately, much of the assistance these children receive will be with isolated drill activity, using flash card drills or games. There is an abundance of such material available for these kinds of activities. This approach poses several large problems. A deficit or weakness emphasis is used. The students are drilled on a group of words that are largely unknown, and the opportunity for success is quite reduced. After witnessing more than occasional instances of such practices, seldom was even modest progress in learning the words observed. Children who are less efficient in learning to read are given the least efficient teaching approach.

The meaning or meaningfulness of these words must be provided by their context in phrases and sentences. The phrase **these dogs** makes the use of **these** far more concrete, and each repetition in such an association represents a larger step toward mastery than does its repetition in isolation.

For high imagery words, many meaningful repetitions can occur quite naturally: verbs and other words on traffic signs, names of familiar stores, restaurants, restroom signs, etc. Picture dictionaries utilize the high imagery word with its referent picture combination. However, no one would ever expect to see a sign that said **where, these, there, as, some, because** or **are.** Again, children who are having the greatest difficulty learning to read are likely to get this less meaningful exposure and repetition.

The need for repetition by these children is not often appreciated. The typical program of instruction in beginning reading does not provide for it.

There is another factor that is also unappreciated: the phonic regularity of words. A word's decodeability, does not reduce the requirement for repetition to learn it. In other words, the fact that a word is decodable because its letter sound associations are accurate, does not lessen the required number of repetitions it needs for mastery.

Imagery level is the most important quality of words when determining need for repetition. This is true primarily for practice given in activities where words are isolated.

At this point, the distinction between **word recognition** and **word identification** should be made. The difference between the two concerns the degree of familiarity of printed words. The term **word recognition** implies instant recognition of a printed word. Word recognition implies familiarity. **Word identification** on the other hand is the process of figuring out what a printed word is. This process may be referred to by terms like decoding, phonic analysis, word attack or word identification. Word identification is useful while the process of becoming increasingly familiar with words is underway. Remember; the fact that a student can use word identification skill to figure out a word, in no way reduces that word's need for repetition before it is sufficiently familiar to recognize instantly.

Word calling is a behavior associated with limited word recognition ability. A word caller overly depends on the word identification process to figure out what all of the words are that he is reading orally. He will read laboriously, word-by-word, "sounding out" or "calling" each word as he tries to figure out how to pronounce it. Reading programs that emphasize word identification skills, without providing instructional and independent level reading activities that supply the critical repetition, foster word-calling behavior (Hargis, 1982).

When children begin to demonstrate deficiency in reading achievement, the assumption is often made that they need additional word identification skill training. Consequently, increasing portions of the curriculum for these children is devoted to just that. This training is often separated from instructional level reading activities. So, the very children who require even more meaningful repetition of words will actually get less.

The primary source of reading activity and consequently the primary source of word repetition is the basal reader. The vast majority of children use basal reading programs when they begin reading. The amount of repetition they supply is sufficient for most children, if they are also getting some repetition of the same high frequency words in other activities. However, the amount of repetition the basal readers supply is totally inadequate for lower achieving students (Hargis, 1982; 1985). Words are not systematically repeated in basal readers once they are introduced. The repetition that they do receive is quite inconsistent.

When words do not get sufficient repetition, increasing numbers of them remain unfamiliar. This increasing load of unknown words makes the material too difficult for instructional purposes. To make a book readable, supplementary teacher-made material must be supplied to provide the necessary repetition of the many words that have remained unfamiliar.

Research on word repetition (Hargis, 1985) shows that the decodability of a word does not affect its requirement for repetition to become familiar. Decodability makes little difference in learnability of words. That is to say, a phonically irregular word will become part of a students word recognition vocabulary as rapidly as a phonically regular one, if the words otherwise share the same imagery characteristics. The place in learning to read, where word identification skill does help with decodable words, is while repetition is still required. Unfamiliar words must be identified over and over again in order to become familiar. Decoding is useful in working independently to get the repetition needed to recognize words instantly.

Decoding is only one method of identifying words. Children will need various kinds of assistance to identify words that are still unfamiliar. The use of context is probably the most universally helpful in identifying words and can complement decoding ability. Also, a tutor, whether teacher, peer, computer or tape recorder, can supply the word for the student while he still does not recognize it and can't independently identify it. Any of these procedures constitute methods of supplying the necessary repetition. The important thing to remember is that what these children require most but are least likely to get, is adequate repetition within an instructional level of difficulty.

What they are more likely to get is more work on isolated word identification skill training. However, word identification skills can only be efficiently applied if unknown, decodable words appear in the context of reading selections and activities that are at an instructional level of difficulty. Therefore, excessive word identification skill training has limited benefits with LD and LA children. Teachers are often heard to say something like, "He knows his phonics, but he still can't read." This should be less surprising than it is. Remember, successful students are applying their word identification skills in instructional level reading activities. The unknown words appear in sufficiently rich contexts and with reasonable frequency. These same conditions are just as necessary for lower achieving students.

Repetition is an extremely important factor in improving the reading ability of LD and LA students. The amount of repetition required is not often appreciated. The need for repetition is overlooked because we tend to think that reading deficiency is the result of a subskill deficiency in the student and not the result of a deficiency of repetition of words in the reading material. The assumption may be made that the repetition provided is adequate formost students, so it is adequate for all students. If this is so, then the source of the problem must reside elsewhere. Also, our current diagnostic testing procedures direct our attention away from curricular materials and to the student. However, the deficiency is not in the student; it is in the reading material.

The repetition requirement that have just been discussed apply to beginning reading activities. Attention to the need for extra repetition is extremely important for slower students. However we have good evidence that the need for extremely large amounts of repetition lessens as the students acquire skill and fluency at reading.

Repetition at the Instructional Level

Words are best given repetition at the instructional level. Instructional level reading gives the student an opportunity for real repetition of as yet unfamiliar words. At the instructional level, context is sufficiently rich to assure that identification of the unfamiliar is made. At the frustration levels, context will be less and less helpful as the number of unknowns increases. Remember; if a word is not identified, its occurrence does not count as a repetition. Real repetition occurs only when a word is identified. It is useless to repeat a word without identification.

There are a variety of ways in which words can be identified for real repetitions. Someone can tell a student what an unknown word is. When a student encounters an unfamiliar word, the teacher, tutor or parent can identify the word for the student. Context alone can be sufficient help in identifying many words. This context can be linguistic or nonlinguistic. Reading selections at the instructional level provide good linguistic context. Words that label things receive this context from the thing that they label. This kind of context is very helpful at beginning reading levels. As a student acquires decoding skill, he can couple the use of context with this emerging skill to identify unfamiliar words. Again the use of decoding skill is most efficiently and effectively applied in reading material which is at the instructional level.

Instructional level reading can be thought of as a guided drill. The material itself provides good supporting context for the identification of words. Decoding skills can be efficiently applied at this level. Children should not be burdened with word identification. When too many words are unfamiliar, reading becomes a painful word-at-a-time reading that fosters the word-calling behavior that was described earlier. Success at word identification is as important as success is in all other aspects of instruction.

Instructional level reading activities should provide the bulk of the repetition requirements for most children. With a manageable burden of unfamiliar words, students can work independently with minimum amounts of guidance. This is very important when working with large groups of students and with a minimum of extra help.

Conclusion

Word introduction and word repetition are the primary considerations in providing reading materials and activities that produce achievement in reading. In their correct measure, they provide instructional level reading activities for individual students. Observation of students while reading, provides the basic assessment information as to whether the rates match the needs of particular students. The specifics of these assessment techniques will be described in chapter 6.

CHAPTER 5

INSTRUCTIONAL LEVELS AND RATES
IN ARITHMETIC

$\mathbf{A}$ S WITH reading instruction, the balance of unknown to familiar
constituents determines the instructional level of an arithmetic activity. The ratios are different and the requirements for repetition can be
more varied. This will be the subject of this chapter. The levels of difficulty being sought are, however, intended to produce the same effect as
in reading. This effect is maximum on-task time, success and achievement. The numbers that will be discussed are the basis for making an instructional match between curriculum and student. Again, the match
between a student and the curriculum must be made very specifically. It
is made in the daily arithmetic activities that are used to achieve curricular goals. These daily activities are where the student must have instruction to produce success and on-task time. CBA is the matching process;
instructional levels and rates are the criterion indexes that show the accuracy of the match.

Assessment that maintains the instructional level match is routine. It
is a part of all the assignments and drill activities in which the students
engage. It is checking the work, not with giving a grade in mind, but
with determining the accuracy of the match between the difficulty of the
activity and the skill of the student. Always, the teacher should be striv-
ing for the same range of scores. These scores are the numbers which say
the instructional match has been made. In classrooms where CBA is
used, the scores on assignmens will be quite uniform; only the material
and activities on which the scores are given will vary. This is quite different from the typical classroom where the scores vary greatly, and the
materials and activities are uniform in difficulty level.

The level of a student's performance on a specific assignment determines its instructional level for that student. This level of performance is compared to standards that indicate the instructional level in arithmetic. If there is a gap between the student's performance and this standard, then an adjustment in the difficulty level of the assignment should be made.

Instructional Level in Arithmetic

Appropriate instructional levels in arithmetic are produced by manipulating the introduction rate of new items and then the repetition of the items once they have been introduced. At any given time, the ratio of knowns to unknowns in the instructional activity will determine its appropriateness. New items must be introduced, repeated until they are mastered, and steadily replaced by new items; so that progress along the curriculum is maintained.

How much new information can be introduced at a given time? In Miller's (1956) classic article, limitations of memory appear to hold this to about seven "pieces" plus or minus two. In introducing new items in arithmetic, the issue is more complex than this relatively simple storage example. It comes fairly close, though, when less complex items such as counting and basic facts are presented. This of course can be true only if the student has the readiness skills basic to the presentation of the new items. The important thing to remember is that there are limitations on the amount of new information that can be introduced. Additionally, when planning drill activities, the relative newness of the item may add some memory burden. The fact that an item has been introduced previously and has been subject to some drill does not mean that it cannot contribute difficulty. Certainly, if a student encounters so much unfamiliar material in some drill activity that he can no longer stay on-task or have a reasonable level of success, it has too many unknown or unfamiliar items on it. If a student encounters more than about 25 percent new or unfamiliar items on a worksheet for example, he will have difficulty staying on-task and demanding extra teacher help in completing the activity (Gickling and Thompson, 1985). A range of about 15 to 25 percent new or unfamiliar items in mixed drill activities is about as much as a student can handle without going off-task. It should be remembered that these percentages are of things that have been introduced. The student should have some idea of how to deal with them from an initial introduction by the teacher or by its placement in some helpful context. In isolated drill activities, it is likely that all of the drill focuses on the newly introduced items. Here again the activity will be attention maintaining only if the student has had careful introduction to the new items.

In the mixed drill activities about 75 to 85 percent of the items should have been subject to previous drill and should be in various stages of mastery. They are being reviewed for mastery, fluency, accuracy or maintenance. How does the teacher monitor the appropriateness of the introduction rate for individual students? This is done quite simply by checking accuracy of responses which should be in the range of 75 to 85 percent.

These scores indicate the appropriate mix of new and review items have been managed. They are fundamental consideration in managing success and optimizing achievement. This notion is at times hard for some to accept. It means that all students should be getting essentially the same scores on their work in math most of the time. This is a fundamental change. Instead of using about the same arithmetic material with all the students, thereby producing pronounced variation in scoring; the difficulty level of the material is varied to individual need, thereby producing uniformity in scoring. Remember, this does not mean there is uniformity of achievement. The achievement levels will remain quite varied but higher than under the old system.

With curriculum based assessment, the scores which are always sought, must be the same for all students. These scores indicate that a match between curriculum and student has been made at the instructional level. Scores should be the same; the materials and activities should vary. This prevents the curriculum from being a Procrustean Bed.

Repetition Rates

Drill is an important part of math instruction. How much repetition or practice is required for mastery of a skill? Are there any considerations that effect the amount of repetition? What is mastery itself? What levels of accuracy i.e., 60, 80, 90 percent, are indicative of mastery? What role does review play in learning?

First of all, no amount of repetition, no matter how great, will guarantee learning of something if a child is not ready to learn it. Gagne (1970) pointed out that for learning and drill to be effective ". . . a learning program for each child must take fully into account what he knows how to do already. One must find out what he doesn't know how to do already. One must find out what he doesn't know how to do already. One must find out what prerequisites he has already mastered — not in a general sense but in a very precise sense for each learner."

When prerequisite skills are carefully presented and learned, use of drill is much optimized and learning much more efficient. Obviously, a child is not ready for a task if he does not have the prerequisite skills. Drill is not nearly as effective in remembering nonsense items as it is in learning concrete meaningful ones. Math items for which prerequisite skills are missing become nonsense items.

Assuming a child has the prerequisite skills for learning a new item, how much drill will then be required? Resnik and Ford (1981) review research related to the relative difficulty of arithmetic problems and the amount of drill they require for mastery. The early research did not attempt to find why problems were easier or harder. They simply ranked them by what seemed to be their ease or difficulty in learning or the number of trials to mastery. The relative difficulty is likely due, however, to the amount of mental processing involved in specific problems. Loftus and Suppes (1972) predicted problem difficulty by what they called "structural variables" which seem to contribute to their complexity.

The three determinants of the amount of drill required for learning are: Readiness (having the prerequisite skills), the complexity of the computational activity and the concreteness of its original presentation. Unfortunately, on an individual basis, it may take great effort to plan for teaching and drill using all three considerations. Improvement in computer-assisted drill offers promise in removing some drudgery in the preparation of drill activities.

Another consideration in regard to drill or practice is "spacing." It is generally known that "spaced" practice is more effective than "massed" practice for most arithmetic skills. In other words, practice sessions with limited amounts of repetition spaced over several days are more effective than the same amount of repetition concentrated in one period.

Isolated drill and mixed drill activities may be considered at different stages of learning. Extended practice involving similar types of problems characterizes isolated drill, while interspersing various types of problems with other types represents mixed drill. It seems that generally the mixed drill is more productive but that isolated drill is best when a new item has first been presented and needs to be established. Also, isolated drill is a helpful remedial procedure in eliminating habituated procedural errors in particular types of computations. Mixed drill is used for maintenance and mastery.

The ultimate function of drill is to increase fluency or rate of response as well as accuracy. The student who is fluent and accurate has reached the level of automatic response to the computational procedure. Ultimately, this will increase the efficiency in problem solving, because the student can handle many of the computational constituents of the problem automatically, thereby reducing the total memory load and time required to determine the answer.

The important thing to remember about a repetition is that it is the association between a new item and the correct answer. Simply providing a certain number of new items in drill activities for a student does not mean that student is getting that many repetitions of the item. Each time a new item occurs, the correct answer to it must be identified. Unless the correct answer is identified, the occurrence does not constitute a repetition leading to mastery. If the student is identifying an incorrect answer, he may be on the road to learning an item incorrectly. This in turn may require a prolonged remedial effort to unlearn the incorrect response and then learn, to mastery, the correct one.

Real repetitions, where the correct answer is linked with the problem, can be made in a variety of ways. A tutor can supply the correct answer each time the student encounters a new or still unfamiliar item. The tutor might be a teacher, a fellow student, a parent or a computer. The resource of such tutors is not uniformly available, so other provisions need to be made for insuring that a correct response is associated with new items. Massed practice activities which immediately follow a new item's introduction benefit from the short term memory of the student. Real repetition can be provided by placing new items in contexts that are sufficiently strong so as to insure that a correct association is made. Spaced practice then is provided until mastery is achieved. Examples of these activities are given in a later chapter.

Seventy to 80 percent accuracy on daily activities is adequate for keeping a student on task, but the items missed must still be corrected. The students must have these missed items corrected; the sooner the better. Routine correction of tests and papers is a necessary part of math instruction. The correct repetition must be made. The correction of papers will supply some of the repetition need for mastery. It doesn't do any good simply to mark items wrong. A good repetition requires making a correct response. The students must see the correct response for all of the items missed before they have the chance to respond incorrectly again.

What level of accuracy is the expected outcome of drill? Ninety percent accuracy is evidence of mastery. For the basic addition, subtraction,
and multiplication facts close to 100 percent is desirable but uninten-
tional errors make 90 percent accuracy about the greatest level that can
be expected from children in computational activities. It seems that only
diminishing returns can be expected from continuing drill after this
point. Ninety percent appears to be sufficient to demonstrate mastery in
areas of simple computation. Lesser levels should be accepted in more
complex algorithms where several computational procedures compound
the likelihood of error.

Concreteness and Meaningfulness

The problem of making arithmetic learning meaningful has been a
consideration of educators for many years. On the surface, this important idea may seem rather simple. However, two quite different approaches to meaningfulness have emerged. Very early the drill and
practice of unrelated procedures and facts isolated from application was
criticized. Efforts were made to relate each fact and procedure to practical activities where they were needed in dealing with problems in daily
living, i.e., making change, measuring a room for carpeting, calculating
wages, etc. In this way, use and meaning were equated. This seems to
have been a rational, practical notion.

At the end of the 1950s, a very different approach to meaningfulness
emerged. Now, meaningful learning meant linking underlying structure
and concept with the mathematical fact or procedure being learned.
This approach is an intellectual one in which meaning is related to
knowledge of the structure underlying the fact or process, rather than
meaning being related to a use of the fact or pocess. This is a conceptual
approach rather than a computational approach to arithmetic instruction. Resnik and Ford (1981) have a thoughtful review of meaningfulness in mathematics instruction.

Another way that meaningfulness can be viewed quite apart from the
two views just discussed, has to do with concreteness. This view can be
seen in the following example which presents the concept of place-value.
A concrete set of objects that can be manipulated might be used to find
answers and formulate concepts in regard to place-value. These objects
may be any common, convenient-to-manipulate items such as straws,
blocks, chips, marbles, etc. The number 76 would be represented by
seven sets or stacks of ten chips and one of six. In other words, seven

tens plus the six. The students would be directed to the standard notation for the number which this concrete array represents. This concrete procedure is used to assist in teaching an abstract construct which concerns the number system.

The notion of place value, per se, is not necessary in learning a number. It is also very reasonable to learn to regroup ("carry" or "borrow") without being introduced to place-value. Place-value, however, has much to do with understanding the meaning of mathematical structures, but it is actually more abstract than addition and subtraction with carrying and borrowing, which is the very thing it is supposed to make more meaningful. From may vantage point, with experience working with LD and LA students, it is easier to learn place value well after some of the basic computational skills have been mastered.

Concreteness can and has been used in teaching simple facts and computation directly. Concrete objects can be counted or manipulated as needed to solve immediate problems without ever stopping to deal with concepts or mathematical structures. This is a step closer to reality and is a more sensible approach for those students who cope less well with abstract underlying structure. Counting and computation can be achieved more expeditiously with this direct concrete approach.

In some computational activities, such as extracting a square root, it is difficult to effectively use concreteness as a learning facilitator. Here, for many children, there may be no meaningful purpose to be found for its application in reality, thus making its mastery much less likely. As curriculum items become increasingly abstract or less common in the day-to-day world, this use of concreteness in learning will be less available for use in teaching those items to an increasingly large group of children, and the need to teach such items should be questioned.

Meaningfulness in terms of the structure of mathematics is an interesting curricular area, but it is misplaced when applied to low achieving learners. When it is more difficulty than the thing it is being used to explain, certainly it loses its value.

Concreteness of presentation is important in facilitating learning arithmetic computational procedures. A concrete mode of presentation is helpful when introducing new facts or procedures. Concreteness is better used in introduction than in drill for mastery.

Word Problems

Thought problems or "word" problems pose extra difficulty in arithmetic instruction. The difficulty will be quite apart from that of computation. However, skill in computation will be a necessary but insufficient readiness base for dealing with the solution of thought problems. Additionally, the problems will usually be presented in print, so sufficient reading ability to recognize all the words in the problem will a readiness requirement. When the student has both the computational skill and the reading skill necessary to do the problem, he then must deal with the logical processes involved. Word problems rarely directly state which computational processes should be performed. A student is far more likely to see a word problem of the form (a) than (b): (a) If Joe is six feet tall and Fred is five feet tall, then how much shorter is Fred than Joe? (b) What number is left if you subtract five from six? In word problem situations students must identify a pattern or gain some insight from the printed discourse as to which computational procedure should be used. If skill at seeing these patterns and gaining these insights is to be attained, then teaching must be quite systematic. The computational and reading readiness stages must be in place and then the various patterns representing computational process introduced in concrete and meaningful situations. Once introduced, the problems should receive the same consideration of repetition for mastery as is needed for computational proficiency.

CHAPTER 6

INSTRUCTION WITH ASSESSMENT

REGULAR, direct assessment which is used not for assigning grades but for maintaining students at an appropriate instructional level, must be an integral part of instruction. In order to keep the criterion scores constantly within the instructional range for individual students, the instructional materials used in any given classroom will vary markedly in difficulty and will require continual adjustment. The very work being performed should be used as the primary instrument of assessment. In this way, assessment will of necessity be regular and direct.

The procedures for this kind of assessment are the normal informal procedures teachers often use already, but with CBA, these procedures are incorporated in the routine of instructional activity. This chapter will give attention to the details of these informal procedures, and show how they are incorporated in instruction in a complementary and reinforcing manner. Assessment is all to often viewed as an entity distinct from instruction; however, it must relate to instruction in the most intimate way.

Reading with Assessment

The informal reading inventory is one of the most widely used assessment procedures. In an earlier chapter, Emmett Betts was credited with formulating the details of and the rational for the use of the informal reading inventory. It was in the description of the procedure that Betts discussed the nature of the independent, the instructional and the frustration reading levels. These remain foundation concepts in CBA. The two important reading levels which produce success and achievement are the independent and the instructional level. The two basic indexes needed to determine whether a student is reading at one or the other of these levels are the number of unknown words and the level of comprehension. Information on either of the two indexes can be observed during the routine reading activities. The reading behavior of a student should be observed in this regard any time he reads aloud. If a student stumbles over, misidentifies or can't identify at all, a word in every three or four sentences; then he is probably reading at a instructional level. If a student hesitates over words in every sentence or demonstrates any other word-calling behavior, he is reading at the frustration level. In this latter instance, the student may have good decoding skills but be so preoccupied with the identification of many unfamiliar words that attention to the content of the passage cannot be maintained and comprehension is lost. Oral reading behaviors of the kinds discussed in this paragraph are clear signals that the reading material being used exceeds the instructional level limits, and adjustments in difficulty need to be made immediately.

In routine silent reading activities, the level of comprehension should be checked to make sure that it is staying at or above the 70 to 75 percent level. In directed silent reading activities, questions are usually provided before or after a selection is read. These questions should be used in determining and maintaining the instructional reading level for individual students.

Routinely checking oral and silent reading behaviors in normal reading activities is the most direct use of the informal reading assessment. This information is available and should be used to tune the difficulty level of material to the needs of individual students. This is the most direct use of assessment and the information in routinely available.

This direct use of the informal reading inventory is a departure from the more common perceptions of its purpose. However, it is this direct use that Betts intended. It is ironic that several criticisms of the informal reading inventory concern uses for which it really was not meant. It has little value in determining what reading grade level a child has attained. This is like using an informal inventory as an achievement test. Standardized instruments, especially those that contain graded paragraphs, do this job more accurately.

To make an informal inventory, selections of 100 to 150 words are taken from each reading level from a basal reading series. Usually about ten comprehension questions are prepared for each selection. Starting at what is adjudged to be an easy level, the student starts orally reading the passages. As the passages are read, the oral reading errors are recorded, and the student answers the comprehension questions that follow each selection. The selections on which the student has fewer than 2 percent word errors and attains 90 percent comprehension indicate the basal or independent reading grade level. The instructional level is indicated when the student makes from 2 to 4 percent word errors and attains 75 percent comprehension. If the reading selections were taken from the basal reading series in which the student being tested will be placed, then the use of the inventory is fairly direct. This is a good use of an informal inventory. It is a good procedure for locating initial instructional level placement for new students. The instrument is made up of the actual curricular material in which the student is to be placed.

If, as is too often the case, the inventory is made up of selections taken from a different reading series or is a commercially prepared "informal" inventory; then the use becomes quite indirect. The grade level for selections read at the independent and instructional levels is basically all that can be gained from these types of inventories. Once the grade level is determined, it is assumed that other reading material at the same grade level will be of the same difficulty level. Such is not the case, however, particularly at the primary grade levels. There is no assurance that the selections taken from one basal series are of equivalent difficulty with other basal series at any grade level. Spache (1976) points out that basal readers vary widely between series in terms of reading level at any designated grade level. The indirect use of the informal inventory is a questionable extension of identifying grade-level achievement. A teacher administers the inventory, identifies the instructional reading level, then places the student in a book of the same designated grade level. This placement is considerably better than a chance placement, but it is very likely that the selection from inventory and the selected book differ in difficulty considerably. At the primary grade reading levels, the only accurate use of the informal reading inventory is direct. The selections should be taken from the books available for use with the student. The instructional level match is then made with the material to be used.

Spache (1976) further pointed out that the readability within a book in a basal series can vary widely. Therefore, it is necessary to continually attend to the reading performance of a student once placement has been made. The most direct method is the routine observation of student reading behavior during regular reading activities, using the guidelines for determining oral reading errors and comprehension for an informal inventory. If a student is demonstrating frustration level behavior, the teacher can provide the extra help necessary to get through the difficult spot or make an adjustment in the material being used.

Measuring comprehension is a necessary but often difficult part of determining the instructional reading level. Comprehension is usually measured by preparing comprehension questions for each selection on the informal reading inventory. The questions ideally should measure such things as recall of detail, evaluation, inference and interpretation. However, not all passages lend themselves equally to the formulation of the same kinds of questions. Experience shows that reliable results can be obtained by increasing the number of questions that are formulated directly from sentences in the selection. Consistency in difficulty of comprehension questions and maximum reliability among all the selections can be maintained in this way. This procedure is recommended because of the difficulty encountered in formulating comprehension questions of all the ideal types. Illustrations of questions are included in a later chapter.

Informal assessment of the instructional reading level usually requires oral reading to check word recognition or word identification. The informal reading inventory approach has received considerable criticism because of the variety of ways used to determine oral reading errors. Also, reliable scoring using any scoring procedure may require a tape recorder so that portions can be repeated to assure that all errors are identified and classified. Such scoring procedures are far too cumbersome and difficult to be of practical use for direct routine use of the procedure. For purposes of identifying material for use with a child, some types of word recognition errors are more significant. Since unknown and unfamiliar printed words most directly contribute to reading difficulty, errors that point them out are very important. Gross mispronunciation, substitutions (not simple substitutions of common words that do not affect meaning), hesitations, and refusals (words that a student will not attempt) are the principal indicators of unknown and unfamiliar words. Oral reading errors that indicate unfamiliar and unknown words, together with a reliable measure of comprehension, make informal assessment very helpful in evaluating reading material.

Betts (1946) pointed out that "vocabulary load is one of the most formidable barriers to reading." The percentage of words that can be unknown in a passage at the instructional level may seem rather small (2-4 percent). But remember, this may mean as many as one new word in every other sentence. Relatively few unknown and unidentifiable words have considerable impact on comprehension.

The informal reading inventory approach is the most important procedure for the direct measurement in reading. It is the procedure to use for initial placement in reading materials, and for monitoring and maintaining students at an instructional reading level. However, children may have not acquired sufficient reading ability to read any connected discourse at an instructional level. In these instances, informal assessment may be only simple word-recognition, using lists of words, graded in difficulty by their order of presentation in the basal readers. Words presented in isolation produce more errors than those same ones presented in context, so 70-85 percent accuracy in word recognition and identification is roughly equivalent to the instructional reading level obtained by reading connected discourse. If an instructional level equivalent is found using a word recognition list, then a regular informal test may be begun at that level or below (if there is a level below).

If an instructional level cannot be found and the student recognizes only a small percentage of words on the lowest levels of the word recognition list; then the few words recognized will constitute the basis for the preparation of appropriate instructional level reading material. If the words are selected from a reading series, the remaining unknown words from that series can be presented and repeated until the student has mastered sufficient vocabulary to read instructionally at that level. Methods of preparing reading material using this procedure are detailed in the next chapter.

In addition to attention to the types of oral reading errors and to measuring levels of comprehension, there is another class of behavioral indicators of frustration level reading. These are those that indicate the student is off-task. If a student is distracted from a reading activity by virtually anything, if he is constantly out of his seat, staring into space or daydreaming, the difficulty level of the reading material being used should be examined and adjustments in difficulty made.

The difficulty of oral reading is usually underestimated. This is especially true for students who are at beginning reading levels. The combined effort of attending to meaning while attempting to identify and produce unfamiliar words is very taxing. For this reason, comprehension should be checked after a student has had an opportunity to read silently the selection under question. Oral reading should only be required after the student has had an opportunity to first read the passage silently.

Oral reading is often one of the most used reading activities. It should be used much more carefully. Children who cannot read well orally or those children who are reading at a frustration level may feel a great deal of stress when required to read aloud. The personality range of children varies from shy to gregarious. Shy students may feel great apprehension when they are required to read orally. Teachers should be sensitive to the fear these students feel when required to perform in an oral reading situation. Such students, when repeatedly confronted with these stressful situations, develop negative learned responses to reading that resemble the worst blocking behavior demonstrated by a severe stutterer. In the author's experience, when students with average and above average ability have severe disability in reading, the cause is directly traceable to bad experiences with oral reading. Shy, reticent children should not be required to read orally unless and until they have the confidence to do so. Certainly no student should be required to read orally before his peers unless the material is close to his instructional level and has been read silently first.

Assessment of Word-Identification Skills

The author has grown accustomed to using the term **word-identification skill.** Other common terms include **phonics, decoding, word-attack, word-analysis** and the like. Each of these terms can be further subclassified resulting in terms like **grapheme-phoneme associations, letter-sound correspondence, structural-analysis skills, auditory blending and syllabication.** These skills are included in all reading programs being marketed today. These word identification skills are remarkably different from one another. They are most different in the order in which they are presented. Virtually all reading programs have a scope-and-sequence list of skills which they introduce over several years. Some programs introduce and stress vowel sounds first. Others do the same with consonant sounds. Syllabication, consonant blends, accent or stress rules may receive varying amounts of attention at different times and in different ways. The variety that occurs in reading programs demands consistency in the assessment of the word-identification skills that are included in them. In other words, the testing of these skills should be done with instruments that measure those being presented in the reading program. This is necessary for test validity as was mentioned earlier, and it is also necessary to make sure that the word-identifications skills being taught remain consistent with those emphasized in the reading program. The word-identification skill assessment should be of the skills being taught in the reading program. Tests come from a variety of sources. Some are specifically related to reading and are given to children who are having difficulty in reading up to grade level standards. Increasingly important as a source for tests in recent years, are state mandated "basic skills" or "proficiency" tests. These tests contain their own scope-and-sequence of word-identification skills that are deemed important by the consultants to the states. However, the scope-and-sequence of skills represented on these tests may vary greatly from what is being presented in individual reading programs across each state. Depending on the importance to the students or to the school system on its students passing such tests, it may be helpful to adopt the test as the basis for the word identification skill program.

A large problem when students do poorly on any such subskill test, is that they may receive an additional emphasis on the subskills missed on one of these tests. This emphasis becomes an additional, parallel curriculum. Teaching to the subskill deficiency dominates the reading instructional time. Learning useful word-identification skills is a helpful aid in learning to read, but a program that is dominated by them only dilutes the opportunity to read. Reading itself is the activity which must be most emphasized in order to make progress in reading. Word-identification subskills are not, per se, reading; though some seem to actually believe this. Word-identification skill is only useful in learning to recognize words that are as yet unknown and in gaining the necessary real repetition of words that is required to become completely familiar with them.

All to often word-identification skill teaching is managed as if it were an isolated entity. The teaching of them occurs quite separately from the actual reading that is part of the program. Again, these subskills are useful only in the identification of words so that the necessary repetition of the words can reach a level required for mastery. The subskill teaching should be an integrated and intrinsic part of real reading activities, not a distinct and separate program.

As was mentioned previously, basal reading programs differ considerably in the scope and sequence of word-identification skills that they present. Only those word-identification subskills that you are teaching should be tested. Each reading series has a scope-and-sequence of subskills that are presented over the course of their program. Most also have mastery tests that accompany them. Do not test against exhaustive lists of subskills. Tests that are intended to be all inclusive have been developed. The odds are that a student will miss some of these assumed subskills, and even though they have not been and are not being presented to the student, instructional time may be diverted to the supposed deficit. Instructional time for actual reading should not be relinquished. Remember; achievement in reading is directly related to time spent at reading.

Word-identification subskills are assessed in numerous ways. At times the testing procedure itself is more complex for some students than the subskill the item is intended to measure. For low-achieving and learning disabled students it is very important to keep the assessment procedure simple and consistent. In subskill assessment several considerations must be influences. Are the skills to be tested in isolation or in context? This consideration has several levels. On many tests letter-sound associations are assessed by asking the student to pronounce letters in isolation from words. However, children normally hear words, not fragmented sounds. The placement of letter-sound associations in nonsense syllables occurs on other tests. In still other tests, real words are used to present the letter-sound associations, but the words are isolated. Here, the context of the word is available but sentence context is not. Sentence context appears to be particularly important in providing clues to vowel sounds in words. For lower achieving students, the latter two levels word context and sentence context, are preferrable because the test format is direct enough to measure skill without being overly complex. These procedures are also more like the use of the subskills in real reading activity. The first two levels, isolated letters and letters in nonsense syllables and words, are less like actual use, and in fact may pose difficulties greater than the subskill which is the subject of measurement.

With learning disabled and low achieving students, the simpler formats are better. They can be used to test word-identification skill in whatever curriculum or program is in use. The following examples are offered to show a simple and direct form of assessment using real words.

For testing initial consonant sounds, a multiple choice of printed words is provided for each association to be checked. The following example is for the initial **w**:

>   drove   dove   wove   rove

All of the words in each row should be exactly the same except for the beginning consonant. The printed forms should be new to the student. In each row the child is to mark the word beginning with the same sound that the teacher provides. The teacher would say, "Draw a line under the word that begins with the same sound as in **weed** and **west**."

For final consonants, print a multiple choise of words for each association to be measured. The following example is for final **b**.

cup	cud	cub	cuff

The words in each row should be the same except for the final consonant sound. The teacher says, "Draw a line under the word that ends with the same sound that you hear at the end of **crib** and **rub**."

Tests of initial and final consonant blends follow the same format. The following examples are for initial **spr-** and final **-dge**.

train	stain	sprain	drain
rink	risk	rid	ridge

In the first item the teacher says, "Draw a line under the word that begins with the same sound as **sprout** and **sprinkle**." In the second item the teacher says, "Draw a line under the word that ends with the same sound as **fudge** and **dodge**."

Vowels require a row of words that are alike except for the vowel sound being checked. The following example is for the short **e** sound:

speck	spike	spook	spoke

Two procedures can be used here. The simpler procedure is to say, "Draw a line under the word that you think is **speck**." The more difficult one is to say, "Draw a line under the word that has the same vowel sound that you hear in **pest** and **hem**."

To test common syllables, the following types of items are used. These are examples for **-tion** and **com-**:

attended	attendant	attentive	attention
cemented	compute	candid	control

For the first example the teacher says, "Draw a line under the word that ends with the same sound as **action** and **mention**." For the second example the teacher says, "Draw a line under the word that begins with the same sound as **compare** and **compact**."

The format can be kept consistent for the assessment of most word identification skills. It is simple enough to learn the procedure. Mastery of the subskills can be reliably checked using this format. However, word-identification skills can also be checked as they are used and taught in daily reading activities. Examples of how to prepare these activities are included in the next chapter.

Arithmetic Assessment

When a student gets about 70 to 80 percent of the problems or drill items correct on an activity, he is very likely meeting with sufficient success for it to be attention maintaining and to indicate that progress is being made. However, if the activity is structured so that even more of the items are correct, the practice gained may be more beneficial. Drill and practice is very much a part of arithmetic instruction. Repetition of each newly introduced item is necessary until the student gains familiarity and proficiency at it. Remember; a repetition of an item is only a good repetition or real practice that leads to proficiency, when it is done correctly. Missing items repeatedly can be negative practice. It is important to structure activities so that the students can get the correct answer each time the item appears. Accuracy at close to 90 percent suggests that the repetition and practice being provided is leading to mastery of the items included on the activity.

Attention must be given to errors, so the fewer errors the teachers has to deal with, the less complicated instruction can be. When an error is noted, make sure the student sees the correct answer as soon as possible and additional practice provided as needed. A large part of what is called remedial instruction is devoted to removing error responses that have been learned through practice. Ninety percent accuracy in arithmetic activities indicates that the practice that is going on is good, and that there will be little room for such negative practice.

Here again, the suggestion is made that all students should be getting the same scores on the work they are doing. It should be clear now that the scores children receive on their work are the primary guide to the appropriateness of the instructional activity. This appropriateness of fit is indicated by a fairly narrow band of scores. The arithmetic materials and activities used in a classroom should be varied considerably to fit the variability of the students in any classroom, and the index of having accomplished this is the uniformity of scores.

There are several levels of instructional activity in arithmetic. The initial level of instruction is when the new item is introduced. The practice that should follow immediately capitalizes on the short term memory of the student. The impression of a clear concrete illustration of the item sustains the student through the massed repetition of the item. If the student cannot successfully perform drill activities at this level, the introduction should be simplified or readiness for learning it should be checked and a lower level of instruction identified. The practice that follows provides for the acquisition of the item as it is nudged into the long term memory of the student. The next level provides practice for increased proficiency and fluency. The last level is mastery or automaticity. Students will vary considerably in the amount of repetition required to move through these levels. An important part of assessment becomes the attention to the amount of repetition required for mastery. Checks on speed and accuracy can be used to determine mastery of various arithmetic facts or algorithms. Even at mastery levels, fluency or speed of response is a quite variable thing. Considerable leeway should be provided. It should be viewed in terms of the change in fluency from the time of introduction to the time of mastery. There is no absolute standard.

If a pattern of error has been established this response pattern must be broken. Correcting error patterns is a remedial activity. Developmental work at an instructional level should produce skill without producing error patterns. However, these patterns may emerge because of a missing subskill, performing a wrong operation, or development of a faulty step in complex algorithms. Students' work should continually be monitored to prevent the recurrance of errors that permit error patterns to develop.

The following example should serve to illustrate a rather common pattern. A resource teacher was asked to help a student with subtraction. He just couldn't understand it. The child's regular classroom teacher couldn't fathom the type of mistakes the child seemed to make consistently. Given a set of computational activities in subtraction, the student produced these answers:

$$
\begin{array}{ccccc}
15 & 8 & 7 & 6 & 10 \\
-7 & -3 & -2 & -5 & -7 \\
\hline
15 & 8 & 7 & 6 & 10
\end{array}
$$

The resource teacher was baffled, so she asked the student to tell her how he was doing the problems. The student explained, "I am doing exactly what my teacher said. If I take away the bottom number, what number will be left? Only the top one is, so I write it under the line." The errors shown above are the literal interpretation of insufficient instructions. The reason for the error is relatively simple in light of the explanation, but reasons are not always as apparent as this case shows. The most direct assessment procedure for determining the cause of an error pattern, if it is not readily apparent, is to ask the student how he is doing the problem.

The reader is well referred to Ashlock's (1986) work for assistance in learning to identify error patterns so that remedial activities can be directed specifically to their elimination.

It takes almost as much time to learn an error pattern as it does to learn the correct pattern of response. However, the error pattern will require instructional time to eliminate; and then additional time will be needed to learn to do it correctly. These are additional reasons that scores on instructional activities in arithmetic should be kept quite high for all children. It not only insures success, but it also insures the instruction is efficient.

General Assessment

The bulk of the discussion of assessment has been devoted to reading and arithmetic. Other curricular areas do have special problems but the general guidelines for arithmetic or reading often apply. In teaching handwriting and spelling the same standards used for drill and practice in arithmetic can be applied. In various content subject areas, reading is the vehicle of instruction and so the difficulty of the reading material should be adjusted to within the instructional level guidelines. Beyond this, specific information is presented and is to be learned. Assessment should still be drawn directly from the instructional activity. Indirect means of assessment lose validity, and may become more difficult than the concept or content they are intended to assess.

Of all the curricular areas, the most difficult and subjective one is written expression. There are no simple standards represented by numbers or percentages here. The author has attempted to impress upon the reader the great amount of individual variation that is to be found in academic ability in any classroom. If anything, this range of differences is even greater in language production skill. It is therefore necessary to find a reasonable starting point for each student where success can be attained and progress continued. In the same classroom successful written expression may range from only a one word response, to a query, to the ability to summarize rather complex events and even produce a short story. It is important to develop instructional objectives for students given these many different ability levels. The objectives should be formulated given where the student is starting, and then choosing the next more elaborate means of expression. When a student attempts to write creatively and beyond refined means, papers should be scored only with the appropriate instructional objectives in mind. Students should always be reinforced for making these more elaborate attempts. An environment which fosters written expression is important. When a student sees his writing efforts covered with red marks, the effort is soon withdrawn.

Assessment attention on these works should be directed to the student's progress on the limited set of specific objectives that he is quite likely to achieve and to which instruction is being directed.

Conclusion

The bulk of instructional assessment should not be used for giving grades. Grading is an issue that will be quite different from the routine of assessment and this topic will be the subject of a later chapter. Assessment's primary use should be in tuning the curriculum to the individual student's needs. Remember the ax and rack of Procrustus? Keep in mind that it should be directed to making adjustments in the curricular bed, not adjustments in students.

CHAPTER 7

THE PREPARATION AND SELECTION
OF MATERIALS

THERE IS NO particular method or approach to teaching advocated with curriculum-based assessment. The system should work compatably with the various methods of teaching reading or math and even with approaches that are directed to different sensory modalities or learning styles. CBA is not a method in the conventional sense. However, CBA is a system of relating assessment to instruction. Regardless of method, it is a system of maintaining individual instructional levels in order to produce success. Consequently, it is also a system of individualizing instruction in that it matches the instructional difficulty of materials to the individual.

Direct Assessment

The most direct form of assessment occurs when the instructional material in use is itself used as the assessment device. This is so whether the assessment is for initial placement at an appropriate point on the curriculum, or is for the ongoing adjustment of material that is required as progress along the curriculum is made. However, for many students, their skill and achievement level may be so limited, that no instructional material can be found that matches their instructional needs. For these students, it is virtually impossible to find readily available instructional material that is suitable. In these cases, both the assessment procedure and the resultant instructional material will be reduced subdivisions of the more complex instructional material that is closest in difficulty on the curriculum sequence. Assessment and instruction then will be directed toward getting the students up to this entry level on the curriculum. For example, a new second-grade student is given passages to read from the primary levels of the basal reading program. Even at the pre-primer level, he can identify fewer than half the words. It is clear that even the lowest reading level available will be much too difficult for the student to use with success. The assessment procedure to use at this point is aimed at finding what word recognition skill the student does have with the basal vocabulary, so that a lower starting point can be identified. This starting point will be used to proceed to the mastery of a sufficient amount of the basal vocabulary so the student can read the preprimer at an appropriate instructional level.

Remember, the focus of assessment is on strengths. Instructional activities must be comprised largely of things that are possible for the student to do. For children who have become curriculum casualties, it may be a challenge to find some strength or skill to use as a starting point; then given such a small base, it may be an additional challenge to prepare materials and activities that they can do. But it is quite possible to do so, and some simple methods of assessment and preparation of materials that have been used repeatedly and successfully with these students will be illustrated shortly.

Teachers have grown increasingly dependent on published materials. For low-achieving students, however, it is often next to impossible to find published material that matches the need at these lowest levels. This will be particularly so as the student gets older and his skill level remains quite low. Now the problem is confounded by the lack of age appropriateness in the lower ability level of materials. When age appropriate material is found, it often will not attend to the objectives of the specific curriculum in use. To make certain that the material is valid in regard to the curriculum and suitable for particular students, it is often, of necessity, teacher made.

As reading skill increases, it will be more and more likely that conventional published material can be found that is instructionally appropriate. In addition, when a student reaches a high second grade or third grade reading level, it will be possible to find books that a student can read that are within the student's level of achievement. The matching approach can be more correlational and less direct.

Preparing Reading Material

Teachers feel most helpless when they encounter students for whom none of the available instructional material seems to work. "I just can't find anything for him to do," is a common complaint. Many teachers feel that it is beyond their expertise to prepare reading material if the "experts" who write all this wonderful stuff that works with the rest of the students cannot. The hard facts are that you are unlikely to find appropriate published material, and that you will very likely have to prepare a good deal of it yourself. The comforting facts are that it is possible to prepare it yourself and the task is not as formidable as it would seem.

The first task that needs to be done is to find what words, if any, a student has learned. Reading material that is comprised of mostly known words will need to be prepared using these words. The most likely place to find known words is among the words that make up the material that the student has been working in. Even though he obviously does not know enough of the words to read any of the material at anything other than a frustration level, he is fairly likely to have learned at least some of the more concrete or frequently occurring ones. Starting with the lists of words from previously used basal readers or remedial material, simply inventory the known or identifiable words. With students who are still fundamentally nonreaders regardless of their age, it is less frustrating for them to be tested from lists or flashcards. Since they have so little reading skill, they would not benefit from the use of context in identifying most of the words anyway. If the words are tested in isolation, the students will not need to be exposed to the painful process of trying to red frustration-level passages.

The number of words so identified may seem painfully small. There are other sources from which familiar words may be found, if the pool of words does not provide much to work with. Children may have learned to recognize the names of fast-food products, chain stores, and the signs and labels of commonly encountered items in their environment. Quite often they will recognize their own name and even the names of other students. Any additional words will be helpful in the preparation of beginning reading materials for these students. The following list of known words was identified with an eight year old who apparently had made no progress in reading.

preprimer		*primer*		*1st grade*
a	I	this	he	of
and	is	to	no	or
big	it	up	on	*2nd grade*
blue	look	we	ran	hot
can	me	you	so	off
for	my		too	

get	red	two
go	see	yes
help	the	

With such a few words to work with, it would seem nearly impossible to prepare any kind of reading selection let alone written at an instructional level. But it is possible, and it is not as difficult as it would seem from the alphabetical list of words from the four levels that are shown above. A more suggestive pattern of use can be made if the words are organized by part of speech and then placed in positions close to where they would occur in common simple sentences.

a	Joe	can	get	me	and	big
the	I		go	it	or	blue
this	it		help	you		hot
my	he		is			red
			see			two
			look			
			for	yes		
			to	so		
			up	too		
			on			
			of			
			off			

Notice that this student could not recognize any nouns other than his own name. This meant that some new words that were nouns would have to be introduced in the selections being prepared.

Joe sees a bike.
I see the bike.
Joe gets on the bike.
He can go on the bike.
I run to the bike.
I get on the bike, too.
Joe is on the bike, and
I am on the bike, too.
We go on the bike.
Joe gets off the bike.
Joe helps me.
Joe helps me go on the bike.
I can go on the bike, too.

The noun introduced in this selection is **bike.** It was introduced by providing a picture with the caption **bike** to go with the printed story. It was the only unknown word in the selection. This selection was the first that this student had ever been able to read independently. He was surprised and delighted.

Notice that the word **bike** was repeated twelve times in the selection. By rereading the selection on subsequent days, the word will receive most, if not all of the repetition it requires for instant recognition.

In the next selection that was prepared for the student, two new words, the verb **read** and the noun **book,** were introduced.

> Joe sees the book.
> I see the book.
> You see the book.
> Joe gets the book.
> Joe can read the book.
> He reads the book.
> You get the book.
> You can read the book.
> You read the book.
> I get the book.
> I cannot read the book.
> Joe helps me read the book.
> You help me read the book.
> You and Joe help me read the book.
> We read and read.
> I can read the book, too.

The word **read** received twelve repetitions in the selection and **book** fifteen. The words were introduced in a sentence written on the chalkboard. It said, I can read a book. The word **read** was underlined in red, and **book** was underlined in blue. The words were underlined in these respective colors as they appeared in the selection. The use of colors were arbitrary and was only used in the beginning stages of working with the student to make certain that he could readily and successfully identify all the unknowns in these selections.

You will notice that not nearly all of the words available for use in preparing these selections were used. Closer examination of the stories will certainly suggest other ways they could have been written and other sentences that could have been added. Certainly someone else could do a better job. However, these selections were prepared given limited time, to put into immediate use to help a specific student begin reading at the instructional level for the first time.

It can certainly be argued that the sentences are stilted; they are short and choppy; the word use is highly repetitive. Yes, they are certainly all those things and they are repetitive by intent. But one must always keep in the forefront of her mind the fact that the success of the student in reading this material is the foremost objective. It may be necessary to produce such material for lengthy periods until the student has achieved a sufficiently fluent and extensive word recognition vocabulary that enables reading with success in available published materials.

Practice makes it easier to prepare instructional level material for such students. Also, once such selections are prepared, they can be saved and edited for other similarly handicapped students. Even though a student has been in school for several years, it is possible for him to have learned to recognize almost no words with consistency. It is possible to prepare material with an even smaller stock of unfamiliar words than the previous sample. The fewer the number of words a student has in his word recognition vocabulary, the more the teacher will need to use repetition of those words that are familiar and will need to use nonlinguistic context.

The following selection was written for a student who could recognize almost no words with consistency, even his own name. The words **I** and **a** were used because the student recognized the names of these letters, and the names of the letters also represented these letters as words. The verb **see** was used as the new word and thus the verb in all the sentences in the selection.

> I see a boy.
> I see a bike.
> I see a house.
> I see a tree.
> I see a dog.
> I see a cat.

In this selection, the vertical alignment of the words provides clear visual indication of the similarity of the same word below it. All of the nouns are new, so in order to make their identification quite easy, their picture referent was placed beside each. The nouns introduced will necessarily be common concrete nouns that are easily pictured. It is necessary to increase the number of such nouns that a student can recognize as well as the number of common verbs. Even a small stock of such words will make the job of preparing more interesting reading material much easier. As the stock of words is being repeated and added to, the following simple change to the above format has proved helpful:

I see Ed.
Ed sees a boy.
Ed sees a bike.
Ed sees a house.
Ed sees a dog.
Ed sees a cat.

Add the student's name as the subject of an otherwise similar sentence frame. Pictures may be used with the list of nouns again, as needed.

New verbs can be added as in the following selection:

I have a bike.
I have a dog.
I have a cat.
Joe has a bike.
Joe has a dog.
Joe has a cat.

As subjects vary in the sentence frame, the inflectional forms of the verb will change. If the same verb is predictably used in the selection, the change in the subject will make the difference inflected form more identifiable. More verbs are added in this way:

I ride a bus.
Ed rides a bus.
I ride a bike.
Ed rides a bike.

Highly irregular but very important common forms can be handled the same way.

Elsie is a girl.
Ed is a boy.
Joe is a boy.
Mary is a girl.
I **am** a boy.

The definite article, **the,** can be introduced in a predictable context. The introduction of the definite article will make the reading selections less like lists of independent sentences.

A boy rides a bike.
The boy has a dog.
The boy has a cat.
The boy sees Joe.
Joe sees the boy.

The prepositions **in, on,** and **at** are very helpful in varying simple sentence structure. These can be introduced in strong contexts to enhance their predictability. A picture can be used to illustrate the entire sentence to show the preposition in respect to its meaning:

A dog is in a house.
A cat is on the house.
A boy is on a bike.

A few common intransitive and transitive verbs should be introduced early. The action verbs **run, jump,** and **walk** are very helpful. A few adjectives such as **big, little, happy,** and **angry,** as well as some color words can make the selections more interesting and easier to write. Past tense forms of the verbs can be introduced by simply changing the selections already used.

Only simple sentences can be prepared with such limited word lists, but that will be quite satisfactory for the time being. Remember, the student's success is the foremost objective, and the more success he experiences the faster the stock of words will increase. Then the material can be more varied. With the few words introduced so far, selections such as the following can be prepared:

A boy had a dog.
The boy was in bed.
The dog jumped on the bed.
The dog licked the boy.
The dog ran.
The boy saw the dog.
The dog was happy.
The boy ran.
The boy was happy.

As the student's stock of words increases more direct attention can be given to introducing words that comprise the basal vocabulary or the vocabulary of a reading program that you would like him to use. When the student has become sufficiently familiar with enough words, he then can benefit from the instructional use of that material directly.

Experience stories can be used with considerable benefit at the early level of instruction. The language will certainly be familiar to the student, and these stories are much easier to prepare since the number of different unfamiliar printed words need not be as controlled. Also, it is often possible to introduce particular new words into activities that go into experience stories. When a student rereads the experience story, his familiarity with it makes the identification of the unfamiliar printed words much easier. The repetition derived from rereading experience stories is quite possibly the most important benefit derived from this activity.

Providing Adequate Repetition of Words

It is extremely important to provide printed material that a child can read, but it is equally important to provide sufficient repetition of new words in this material so that progress is made in expanding his word recognition vocabulary. Gates's (1930) guidelines for repetition of words are fundamentally sound. The average student requires about 35 repetitions of most words before he can recognized them instantly. Slower students require even more. Repetition of words can be achieved in several ways. In the selection illustrated above, multiple use of each word was nearly necessary because there were so few known words to start with, but even so, multiple use of words may have to be planned for more systematically for the slower students. These students are much less likely to get the incidental repetitions of even those words with the highest general frequency of occurrence. Rereading activities provide an excellent source of repetition of words, and if there are several appearances of the same word in a selection, the student will benefit even more from the rereading. Written comprehension questions that are very simply and directly related to the selection can be used to repeat virtually all the words that occurred in the selection.

Listening to a tape recording of a selection while following its printed text is also an activity where the student can get considerable good additional repetition of a great many different words. The selection need not be made up of largely known words, but the words in it should be unknown only in print. The student can listen and read along repeatedly until he has learned all of the selection and can recognize all of the words when presented in isolation. The more within text repetitions each word has, the fewer reading/listening repetitions the student will need to master the selection. The student will need some basic readiness skills to use this activity. He will have to understand the left-to-right, top-to-bottom tracking procedure required in reading. He will have to recognize what a word and its boundaries look like in print. Even then, the beginning reader may require some help and practice in keeping his place as he attempts to follow the text. Visual and auditory clues may be needed at first to assist the student with this activity. It is an activity in which a student who is far behind can catch up on a considerable amount of vocabulary in an activity that is not particularly stressful. One teacher has varied this activity to capitalize on a student's repetitive listening of popular music. The student was permitted to listen to his favorite song, as he memorized its printed lyrics. There were 67 different high frequency words that the student learned to recognize, and he did it quite willingly.

The selection for taping can be chosen because of its interest to the student or it may be chosen from a graded series of material. The selection should contain the necessary vocabulary that a student needs in order to read further, independently. These activities are helpful, supplementary sources of repetition. There is, however, no substitute for the continued opportunity to read at an instructional level.

Remember; the thing that makes a real repetition of a word is its correct identification. The fact that a word appears, with the necessary frequency, before a student accounts for nothing unless he identifies it each of the necessay times.

Skills Teaching

Curriculum-based assessment is normally neutral in regard to the method of instruction used. However, in the event that some method of instruction, is an impediment to a student's achievement of success, some adjustment to this methodology should be considered.

There are many different word-identification programs in current use. They share one characteristic. For the less able students, they are frustrating and counterproductive. The source of this difficulty is the separation of the word-identification skill teaching activities form any actual reading. The reading activities and the subskill teaching are too often treated quite separately. There seems to be the general notion that there will be an automatic transfer of training to real reading once a subskill is learned. The fact is that isolated subskill training is very likely to remain isolated and to be a subskill of nothing. The student will learn the subskills in the format of presentation, but not be able to apply them. The application of the subskill training must be basic to their teaching. Subskills taught from workbooks, games, and worksheets remain fragmented and abstract. They should be integrated with the selections the student is given to read. Subskills not directly applied in this way will not really be learned. If the opportunity to use them with the words that comprise the discourse being read is not planned, the transfer will not occur. The ability to use such subskills by the less able children needs successful practice as much as any other teaching.

Students will need to have appropriate instructional level reading material in which to practice these skills. New words in reasonably rich contexts are successfully identified using appropriate subskills. It is important to have this known context. Too often the student is expected to apply the subskills to identify an unreasonably large number of unknown words. But, the number of unknown words will reduce the benefit of context and place too large a burden on the student. More emphasis on subskills will not make the material any easier for the student. Remember; for success in the application of subskills it is necessary to effectively apply them. When children have trouble reading, there is always the danger that the reading program for them will become increasingly subskill centered. This means that more time will be devoted to learning the subskills in isolation. When this happens, there is no firm ground for rooting the skills teaching and no meaningful way to apply them.

A method of presenting subskills to these children, that insures the most success in their application is called the "intrinsic method." The system was developed by Arthur Gates (1930). The word-identification skills being taught are directed to words that make up the daily reading selections. The new words are presented in prereading activities which point out that the letter-sound feature being taught and which aid in the identification of the new words. The subskills are also featured in activities that follow the selection, including the comprehension questions. Activities that combine comprehension exercise with word-identification skills can end most reading selections. Comprehension and word-identification should be meaningfully integrated. Remember; it is when there is an over emphasis on word-identification skills without the attention to comprehension, that a student becomes a word-caller and does not comprehend what is read. The following examples show some teacher-made comprehension activities that integrate word-identification. They were developed to accompany a short reading selection.

1. What did the boy buy?
   a cap, a ball, a cat, a hat
2. Where did the cat have the kittens?
   under the bed
   under the shed
3. Which kitten did the boy keep?
   Fatty, Blackie, Brownie, Puff
4. Where did the kitten sleep?
   on the box
   on the bed

The comprehension of the story can be checked at the same time that practice with word identification skills is given. The selection of the correct answer requires use of the letter-sound associations that are varied specifically to provide this practice.

Transfer of training is not an issue here, because the exercise is related to an actual reading activity. The word-identification skills being practiced are on the words being introduced. Combining comprehension activities and the subskill training fosters the active use of context and avoids the development of word-calling behavior. Exercises can be structured to focus on any word-identification skill in the curriculum: common syllables, spelling units, inflectional endings, as well as letter-sound associations.

Arithmetic Activities

No amount of repetition will guarantee learning something if a student hasn't the readiness skills to learn. For example, in arithmetic, a student must have the prerequisite counting concepts before he can learn to add or subtract, and he must be able to multiply and subtract before he can start long division. Mastery of the constituent readiness subskills must be measured at each step along the arithmetic curriculum.

Just as important as readiness is the fact that no amount of repetition will guarantee learning something unless the student gets it right at these repetitions. Remember; it is only a real or helpful repetition if the correct answer is linked with the problem. If a student is getting a wrong answer he is getting a repetition of something that is incorrect. He is in fact a repetition closer to learning an error pattern.

A high level of accuracy is important in drill and practice activities in arithmetic. Only in this way can a teacher be assured that an activity is providing good repetition that leads toward mastery. A performance level of about 70 to 80 percent accuracy is adequate of keeping a student on-task with an adequate feeling of success; but 90 percent indicates that good repetition is being achieved, and there is much less opportunity to practice errors.

When a new fact or procedure is being introduced, it should be done as concretely as possible and then followed immediately by massed practice. Massed practice is where the newly introduced items are isolated and practiced. The concrete presentation will secure the item in short term memory for a sufficient length of time so that it can become increasingly embedded through subsequent drill activities. The initial presentation, which is then followed by isolated, massed practice may itself be subject to repetition for slower students.

How many new items can be introduced at one time? Miller's seven plus or minus two (1956) was discussed in an earlier chapter. With academically slower students, the number will be on the minus side. I should add that Miller did not include low achieving students in his study, so the number could be smaller than the five he suggested. Let us say that we are introducing the multiplication facts. How many new facts can we introduce and expect a student to remember long enough to benefit from the massed practice that follows? A teacher will necessarily experiment to find this answer. The maximum number of new multiplication facts that can be introduced, with the student attaining a 90 percent accuracy rate on the massed practice that follows, is the optimum figure being sought. This level of accuracy on the practice activities shows that the student has kept the items in short term memory long enough to benefit from the repetition.

The initial repetition is provided through isolated drill with the new items being massed together. Subsequent repetition is spaced and mixed with previously introduced items that are being practiced for fluency and mastery.

Drill, practice, repetition; whatever its name, it seems to have a bad reputation. Its careful management, however, is fundamentally important. It is where the problems which require remedial effort begin. The computer age promises the technology for providing repetition as carefully as it is needed without quite so much time and effort in its preparation.

During the practice stages when addition and subtraction facts are being memorized, a variety of formats may be encountered. When the format goes from left to right it is called a sentence. Sentences for addition often look like:

$$6 + 3 = \underline{\hspace{1cm}}, \quad \underline{\hspace{1cm}} + 3 = 3, \text{ and } 6 + \underline{\hspace{1cm}} = 9$$

Sentences for subtraction look like:

$$6 - 3 = \underline{\hspace{1cm}}, \quad \underline{\hspace{1cm}} - 3 = 3, \text{ and } 6 - \underline{\hspace{1cm}} = 3$$

The vertical form of notation $\underline{+3}^{6}$ for addition and $\underline{-3}^{6}$ for subtraction are also used in practice activities. In my experience, variation in format may pose more learning difficulties than the facts themselves. When the facts are at the practice stage we recommend that only one format be used. The only sentence form that could reasonably be used is $6 + 3 = \underline{\hspace{1cm}}$ or $6 - 3 = \underline{\hspace{1cm}}$. The other forms can be very confusing. The symbols "$-$" or "$+$" will strongly suggest that subtraction or addition should be performed, but this will not be the case in the other sentence formats. The vertical form of notation will be used for virtually all the longer addition and subtraction problems. So, it seems a sensible way to begin. At any rate be consistent; don't introduce confusing variables at the practice stage with students who have learning problems.

Remedial Instruction

Instruction works best when it proceeds developmentally along the curriculum. When progress goes awry, instruction becomes remedial. Progress along the curriculum may be stopped because of a skill deficiency or an error pattern that impedes learning. The problem that is preventing progress will have to be identified, and then the problem itself will become the focus of instruction. The problem will become the curriculum. This will be necessarily so until the error pattern or skill deficit can be removed and normal progress resumed. If the remedial program is not undertaken, there is the danger that the student will be further practicing his problem and thereby compounding it.

To avoid problems which require remedial attention it is important to make sure that success rates on instructional activities are quite high. This is good insurance that skills are emerging and error patterns are not. When errors appear that seem consistent, then some remedial action should be taken promptly. Remedial instruction is necessary, but it is replacing developmental instructional time.

When a student is clearly disabled by such problems, it may be necessary to review his performance diagnostically. There may be an array of problems that need attention. This leads to a major pitfall in remedial instruction — the over-emphasis on deficits or problems.

When assessment is diagnostic, the diagnostician is looking for problems and deficits. When they are identified, a remedial program focusing on them will be prepared. This is fundamental to the diagnostic-prescriptive model. The pitfall is that a program focussing on deficits or problems can be frustrating and nonproductive. Remember; success should be emphasized even in remedial instruction. It is difficult to keep this in mind when the diagnostic effort is on problems and deficits.

When a remedial program is undertaken, it is just as necessary as ever to balance it heavily on the side of a students strength. The ratio of knowns to unknowns should remain the same as for developmental instruction. The same levels of success and comprehension should be shown in the students performance.

A secondary problem with remedial instruction is that it has the tendency to focus on isolated subskills. This is particularly true in reading. With low achieving students, one is likely to be disappointed if a transfer of training is expected from an isolated activity to actual reading performance.

Diagnostic tests should reflect the content of the curriculum in use. If deficits are identified that are not a part of that curriculum, the information may actually be trivial. Unfortunately, it is likely to receive remedial attention anyway. This will only dilute the time that is spent on the regular curriculum. This speaks to the importance of using valid diagnostic measures, measures that are related to the student's regular curriculum.

CHAPTER 8

IDENTIFYING LEARNING DISABLED STUDENTS

T HE TERM, "learning disability," was first used by Sam Kirk (Hallahan and Kauffman, 1986) in 1963. It was an attempt to provide a unifying label for a myriad of terms associated with children who have difficulty in learning. The many terms that are subsumed in this category imply some degree of brain abnormality and all imply a defect that resides within the student. The term learning disability focuses the attention on the learning problem rather than on the variety of confusing labels that implied some cause. However, even the label, learning disability, implies that something is wrong with the student, and that the cause of the learning problem is within him. Throughout this book, the curriculum, rather than the student, has been emphasized as the cause of most learning problems.

In many states, a discrepancy definition is used to determine if a student can be classified as learning disabled. It has been concluded in these instances, that a student can only be meaningfully classified as learning disabled, if there is a significant discrepancy between his capacity, or potential for learning, and his actual achievement. The size of this discrepancy is usually in the order of one standard deviation difference between potential and achievement. Sometimes the discrepancy is stated in terms of grade-years of achievement, depending on the age of the student. There are several reasons discrepancy has become popular in verifying the existence of a learning disability. It avoids the use of cause in the identification. There are so many subjective notions as to cause that confusion usually results. However, the main reason may well be that a disability cannot really exist if it has not had a significant, negative impact on learning. It ultimately doesn't matter if the child demonstrates some symptom associated with learning disability, if he is achieving as well as he can.

My objection to discrepancy definitions of learning disability is that they require a student to fail to achieve for a sufficient length of time so that a discrepancy emerges. A student may have to endure considerable failure time before a significant discrepancy appears and some help provided. For many children who are simply low achievers, it can take several years of painful nonachievement.

Identification of Learning Disabled Students

Most learning disabled students are quite normal children. The cause of their problem is outside them; it is in the curriculum. Nonetheless, there are children whose problem does exist within them. They are a definite minority, but they need careful attention.

In order to separate "real" learning disabled students from the far more common curriculum casualties, one must discover whether their particular behavior is the result of, or the cause of failure. To do this, it is necessary to provide instructional activity which is clearly within the students ability level and then observe the students' subsequent behavior.

When children do not have appropriate instructional-level material to engage their time, other behaviors appear. Certainly when a student is not engaged in the instructional activity he must be doing something else. A child who is unable to engage in the work of the classroom engages in off-task behavior. This behavior can take a variety of forms. It can range from quiet mental withdrawal to disruptive acting-out. The negative attitude that emerges may result in avoidance. Frustration-level materials do not permit sustained attention and give rise to such labels as "attention deficit" or "hyperdistractible."

Appropriate rates for introduction and repetition are the critical factors in permitting on-task and engaged time. Appropriate rates also permit success and comprehension. Success is highly reinforcing, and, as Skinner (1972) points out, is enough reinforcement for most people. Material designed to faciliatate correct response produces success.

The act of completing a task can be achieved when the activity is at an instructional level. Hewitt (1980) emphasizes the motivation supplied by successful task-completion. Success and task-completion are the highly motivating results of providing material that is at an appropriate instructional level for individuals.

Appropriate instructional-level material is an essential, but possibly insufficient ingredient, for producing sufficient on-task behavior in "real" learning disabled children. These students have problems outside the curriculum.

The assessment procedure for identifying these students still requires providing them with carefully prepared instructional-level materials. The student's behavior and performance is observed after the material or activity is provided. The observation may have to continue over an extended period while maintaining instruction at this level. Residual off-task behavior under this condition is evidence that the cause of the learning problem resides elsewhere, and must be dealt with specifically. However, whatever remedial action is taken, it does not lessen the need for providing appropriate instructional level activities for the student. It is counterproductive to attempt to change off-task behavior when the task itself does not permit attention maintenance.

Thompson, Gickling, and Havertape (1983) report on the effects of using curriculum based assessment and instruction with children that included a group that were receiving stimulant medication to control their behavior. This group of children were identified as having attention deficit disorders with hyperactivity. The group received both medication and no medication under regular curriculum conditions and under instructionally controlled curriculum conditions. The medication was either Dexedrine or Ritalin as prescribed by the child's physician. Under the no medication condition the children received a placebo in capsules identical to the regular medication. These researchers found that the controlled instructional level was as effective in maintaining on-task behavior as medication. However, the controlled instructional material had the added positive effect of producing significantly greater task-completion and comprehension.

Even when children demonstrate many symptoms or behaviors associated with extreme forms of learning disabilities, the primary intervention should be in providing appropriate instructional level material.

If a student's attention span does not extend to the time of the normally assigned work periods, usually twenty to fifty minutes; the work should be shortened so that the task is within his range of attention. The student needs to experience the reinforcement provided by task-completion. After the student has had consistent experience with task-completion the work periods can be extended.

The attention problem of some students may result from extra sensitivity to distraction. This sensitivity should be managed initially by changing the instructional environment to reduce distraction to within the student's tolerance threshold. Study carrels, quiet areas, or sound proofing may be needed to provide an environment that permits task-completion. At this point, the student's toleration level may be gradually increased to more normal levels.

It is necessary to separate the real learning disabled student from the curriculum casualty so that an appropriate instructional decision can be made. In all cases it is necessary to provide to the instructional level needs of the individual student, but it is also necessary to determine if there is a cause outside the curriculum. The assessment procedure required will be automatic if instructional needs are being met. The residual off-task behaviors suggest further attention is necessary. In some instances the behavior itself must become the focus of curricular attention. In other cases the cause itself may need to be found. For example, a student who is chronically hungry is unlikely to attend well even under optimal instructional conditions. In this case the primary intervention will have to be something like a peanut butter sandwich. Lack of sleep, allergies, and other chronic health problems will also need a noncurricular intervention.

Which Approach

In most cases the curriculum mismatch is the root cause of learning disabilities. However, a student's learning problem may to some extent be within him, or may exist somewhere in the out-of-school environment. Nevertheless, regardless of where the cause lies, the first approach is identifying and providing instructional level teaching. Doing this is not only necessary for adequate achievement to begin, but it is also the necessary basis for the next level of assessment — the observation of behavior at the instructional level. Remaining off-task behavior suggests that the behavior itself will need curricular attention, or that you must look elsewhere for a cause.

When students have spent any length of time at school without making much progress, they often have had plenty of opportunity to practice errors and develop bad habits. With these students, an effort to remediate these problems may be necessary as the first order of work. These problems may so permeate the student's performance, that any attempt at regular curricular work would only provide further error practice.

Remember; remedial work requires the same attention to instructional level as does the regular curriculum. A diagnostic-prescriptive approach is in order, but it should be balanced with the assessment of skills. Diagnosis implies identification of problems and deficits. This is important; but since success at the remedial activity is as important as it is with a developmental approach, the focus should remain on the student's strengths. Finding academic strengths with many students requires more careful assessment than finding problems. Avoid the diagnostic-prescriptive pitfall of assessing and focussing on problems and errors. It can frustrate a student even more.

These then are the approaches to dealing with learning disabled students. They include the approaches that focus on the regular curriculum, either developmental or remedial, or both. They include the approaches that attend to cause. If the student's problem is one of attention and distraction that remains after the first has been implemented, then a curriculum that attends to directly managing the behavior is appropriate. Finally, the last approach is directed at finding and eliminating or ameliorating the cause of learning disabilities which include a variety of possible health or social problems.

CHAPTER 9

OTHER ASSESSMENT CONCERNS

THROUGHOUT this little book a link between the curriculum and assessment has been encouraged. When a test is drawn from the curriculum being used, maximum test validity is insured. A student's progress along the curriculum can be plotted, since the test will reveal what, on the curriculum, has been learned. A student's success can be planned if instruction itself is used as a form of assessment. Performance on all routine instructional activities should be used as primary assessment information. Materials and activities are adjusted so that the scores produced fluctuate within the range indicating the instructional level.

CBA emphasizes instruction as testing. This should be the dominating form of educational assessment. However, teachers will necessarily deal with a variety of other tests and assessment issues.

Testing in General

A substantial amount of the school year is devoted to testing. Hearing and vision tests are routinely given, usually annually in the primary grades. A variety of norm-referenced tests are given, annually. Readiness tests are administered during the kindergarten year, and achievement tests are given thereafter. School systems may have prepared lists of objectives based on their curriculum, and students are tested against these, at least annually. The published basal programs used in most instructional areas often provide skills or mastery tests that are given periodically. Teachers give final and unit tests in order to assign grades. If students are having problems, they will be getting diagnostic tests, and possibly individual IQ tests. Increasingly, proficiency and basic skills tests are being mandated. Quite typically, a lot of testing goes on during the school year.

For many teachers the testing that goes on is, for the most part, simply something that they must manage. It has little relevance to the instruction that they are providing in their classrooms. From the students' perspective, the tests can label them, grade them, or permit them to graduate.

Proficiency Tests

Of the tests currently used, the proficiency or basic skills tests have had the most direct impact on the greatest number of students. The importance of the test is quite clear. If you don't pass the test, you can't graduate.

For many mildly handicapped students, the test has provided a new opportunity. If they can pass, it is possible for them to graduate from high school with a regular diploma, rather than something like a certificate of attendance usually received. The importance of the proficiency test for these students has actually made the test form the content of their curriculum. This is the kind of relationship between test and curriculum that makes for greatest validity. It is the relationship required in curriculum-based assessment. One can only hope that the preparers of proficiency tests have the good judgement to include test items that are relevant to the needs of low achieving and mildly handicapped students.

Critics of proficiency tests claim that these tests are too easy, that they should be more difficult. The critics feel these tests may be further lowering standards. Regardless of what the critics say, I believe that they may make education accessible to a larger number of students than ever before. The skill levels on the test are adjudged to be minimal competency levels, not grade level standards. This is a necessity if low-achieving students are to get a curriculum that reflects limited, attainable academic objectives.

This is not to suggest that these proficiency test objectives should be held for all students. Objectives should be determined by the skills and aptitudes of individual students. Remember; skills and aptitudes vary greatly within each chronological age group of children, and that range of variation actually gets greater as a group of children gets older. The academic aptitude of the most able students far exceeds the level of proficiency tests, and the objectives for them should be appropriately set. Further, the performance of the average member of a chronological age group should not be set as the standard for either the high or the low aptitude members of the group.

Assuming we have a culturally similar group of children, IQ test scores can be used to illustrate the range of academic apptitude to be found in any otherwise randomly assembled group of 30 children of the same chronological age. The range in scores will easily be at least 80 to 120. At age six this produces a range of mental ages of 4.8 to 7.2. Mental age is used here to reflect the academic aptitude of the students. The range is 2.4 years (This assumes also that all the children are at exactly the same chronological age. Actually, in first grade classrooms there is usually at least a full year difference between the oldest and youngest student which will further extend the difference.). At age seven the range extends from 5.6 to 8.4 years. This range is now 2.8 years, and widens gradually each year. By the time this group of children reaches the age of sixteen, the range in academic aptitude is from 12.8 to 19.2 years. The difference between the extremes is now 6.4 years. Therefore, in a group of sixteen-year-old students, we could expect to find students who could be working at the seventh grade level and at the college level. I should add that this would be under optimum conditions in which each student was achieving to his or her potential. Notice that the members of this group with the lowest ability have the academic potential to pass most proficiency tests. Unfortunately, most students like them have not had instructional level curriculum, and consequently seldom make achievement progress anywhere near their potential. Often the curriculum is devoted to making a passing score on a proficiency test, for mildly handicapped students. It would also be very good for lower achieving students. It might make it possible to head off the failure these students invariably experience.

Proficiency tests should be viewed as a basal level of performance for nonhandicapped students and should be improved in this regard. There should be some additional attention paid to their relevance as well. In spite of these shortcomings, they make it possible to have a curriculum which reasonably matches the needs of the many low-achieving students who are not being served.

Purposes of Tests

Tests do have important, useful purposes, if the information provided by them is acted upon. One important purpose would be to avoid failure. Tests can determine if a child is ready to begin reading instruction or to move to a more advanced area of study. A second purpose would be in determining the causes of learning problems. These include organic causes, such as hearing and vision problems, as well as curricular difficulties. These causes, if identified, can be controlled or eliminated. Determining cause requires a variety of assessment devices, but many are in regular use. A third purpose is accountability. Standardized or norm-referenced tests are used here. These tests permit the comparison of individual children or groups of children to those in the general population. Performance improvement over time can also be measured. This information can be used to evaluate the effectiveness of a teaching method, some new materials, a curriculum, an individual teacher or, a school.

The purposes of assessment described in the previous paragraph are appropriate to curriculum-based assessment, and they are an important part of it. However, most testing should be directly related to ongoing instruction, drawn from the curriculum itself. Testing is done through direct observation of performance on the daily activities that are used to reach curricular goals.

Avoiding failure was listed as a purpose with primary importance. Certainly the time to prevent a student's failure is before instruction starts. Americans seem to be in a great rush to start instruction, and once it is begun every effort is made to force students up to grade level standards. The unfortunate result of these practices is the failure of a large number of children.

The measurement of readiness for beginning first grade is important. Actually, it is the lack of readiness that is most important and this information is what needs attention. There are a number of ways this information can be used. A delay in admission to the first grade may be appropriate. This delay could range from a few months to even a year or more. Some children will simply benefit from the time to mature, while others will gain from the extension of readiness activities or the aculturation process that can occur given the extra time.

Reading-readiness tests have received much criticism for their imprecision in predicting reading achievement. Their correlation with reading achievement level at the end of first grade is not particularly great. However, accuracy in predicting level of achievement should not be considered their main use. The most important use of these tests is to identify children who are likely to fail. Most standardized readiness tests do this with considerable accuracy, identifying 80 percent of the children who are not ready.

When using a standardized readiness test, the information should be tempered by teacher judgement. Some children will fail in school because of factors other than abilities sampled by such tests. Teacher judgement along with information on the child's health and family background may be the only means of identifying potential failure.

Low scores on readiness tests should direct attention to other assessment procedures. If hearing and vision testing are not generally required, they should at least be available for those children who show a deficit in readiness.

Program evaluation and accountability needs to be a part of the teaching and testing process. Students' progress should be measured with good quality standardized achievement tests. It is always important to measure progress along the particular curriculum in use, but the curriculum itself should receive evaluation. You cannot always use tests based on your own curriculum. You need instruments which represent a broader view of achievement to insure accountability.

Grading

The main purpose of assessment seems to be in grading students. Like eggs, they are graded with A's, B's, and C's. They are held against a standard—in student's case, one based on the curriculum. I have no great quarrel with the system, when it is applied to students who can get A's, B's, and C's. However, when we use a system that produces failure in a very large percentage of our school-age population, I feel something is wrong. Twenty-five to thirty percent of the students in school are not getting passing grades. Also, 20 to 30 percent of the students that start high school are unable to finish.

I should definitely add that our schools are educating greater percentages of students than ever before. This includes great numbers of handicapped students who had not been able to attend public schools prior to 1975. These are among the major positive improvements in American education.

But we can do better. Failing grades mean that there is a mismatch between the curriculum and student. It really means a failure in the system. Our system should be providing an opportunity to achieve to the individual potential of all students.

The success of a school system is marked by the success of all its students. Failure is more than just the opposite of success; it means that little achievement is being made. Failure is not only unproductive in regard to achievement, it has many negative behavioral consequences as well.

Success is not produced by simply accepting a lower standard for the same work. Success is produced when material and instructional activity is provided that permits a high level of performance. Giving a passing grade to a student on a math assignment when half the items are wrong, is not an acceptable practice.

Scores on assignments and tests should be used to gauge the accuracy of the match that has been made. Remember; it takes a high performance level to indicate the match. Curriculum level and the material provided to teach it should be adjusted to produce the higher performance levels. All students benefit where this kind of instruction is going on.

The concern then arises that grades wouldn't mean anything. Everyone would be getting the same grades. My comment in return is that failing grades only mean that our system is imposing failure on some students. This failure should be viewed as failing on the part of the system. The only measured performance that really means anything is the actual level of achievement a student has attained. Most grades should be replaced by straight forward reports of progress on the curriculum and of performance on norm-referenced achievement measures.

The mark of good teaching, and the best indication that optimum progress is being made by all the students in a classroom, is that student performance is at the same high level on all the work done. I am critical of teaching that produces a great dispersion of grades and scores. This means that little attention is being given to the individual differences of the students.

When testing is used more effectively in instruction, it is not used to produce grades. It is used to continually maintain the instructional level of the materials and activities being provided. This means that the instructional materials are adjusted to produce the scores that indicate the instructional level has been reached. Since the instructional activity itself is the test, it is like changing the test to get the desired score.

Accuracy in matching instruction to students is indicated by the instructional level scores they are receiving. Even though the performance level is the same, the curricular objectives for the students in any given classroom will range over several grade levels. Actually it would be better if curriculum items were not sequenced by grade levels. It adds to the inclination to expect all students in an age and grade to be working on the same curricular objectives. Simply sequencing the items on a curriculum without regard to grade or age would lend support to the idea that students could proceed at their own pace. They would be less likely to be forced into a curricular lock-step with age and grade peers.

If the scores being produced are all in close proximity, it is very difficult to give grades. In the public schools, the elimination of most grades would be no great loss. Achievement is better reported by giving specific information on what curricular objectives the student is working, or by standardized achievement test scores. In the latter case, a student's performance can be compared with others in his age group or grade more accurately and more meaningfully than with the grades.

Should grades ever be given, or tests used, to discriminate? Yes, both things certainly should occur. Tests and grades should be used as the means selecting qualified candidates for the teaching profession, for the medical profession, or to be auto mechanics, to name only a few of the many occupations that need to be selective in regards to apptitude and skill. Nevertheless, children in the public schools should receive instruction that matches their individual needs in order to reach whatever their academic potential is. The public schools need to give each student the best start possible. Grades or discriminating measures should then be used by trade schools and colleges to make sure that only the potentially competent be admitted or complete their training programs.

CHAPTER 10

ADMINISTRATIVE SUPPORT FOR CBA

Group Instruction

THERE IS an almost overwhelming tendency to provide instruction in groups. We group everything; we may call it tracking or grading, but its purpose is to deliver a single level of instruction if at all possible. If some students don't quite fit, we just haven't grouped well enough. We seem to think something is very wrong if we can't teach the same thing to the whole class. We feel a need to denegrate our one-room, ungraded school past. We hope for ever larger consolidations, so that we can place students in ever more similar age and ability compartments.

Individualized instruction is also considered within our need for group structure. When individual instruction is planned, it is aimed at giving some students special attention on the subject the whole class is working on. It is not typically aimed at providing instruction at a student's appropriate individual place on the curriculum.

Remedial instruction also concerns our need for grouping. It is usually directed to helping a student work up to group standards. It is not typically aimed at helping a student work up to his potential.

In past years there was some renewed interest in ungraded programming. It was intended to provide better attention to individual differences. Unfortunately, the primary constituent of these experiments was in the architecture of the schools. The physical changes, "open spaces" did very little to address the problem. The missing rooms and walls could not hide the fact that the same old forms of grouping were going on.

A certain amount of grouping is necessary, but we must shake the idea that grouping can somehow eliminate the need to provide for different levels of instruction in the same room.

The need for grouping results also from the nature of curricula. The form of almost all curricula are dictated by the commercially prepared developmental program which has been adopted. When a school system selects a math or reading program, for example, it is also selecting its curriculum. The material provided in the programs are designed for "average" students. They present day-by-day, week-by-week, and year-by-year instructional activities and materials that the average student can learn with that pace. We attempt to group students so that they will fit the layout and keep the pace dictated by commercially prepared material. The format of instruction dictated by these programs is single-level, group instruction.

Taking Control of the Curriculum

Commercially prepared, developmental programs hold a sanctified position, and have a virtual lock on the curriculum in most elementary schools. Granted, they do well for most children, and they are very helpful in providing to the needs of teachers. However, they should not be held in such esteem. For students who can't meet their normative standards, they cause failure.

Curricula should be assigned to individuals not groups. "Falling behind" or "catching up" are phrases that suggest a student has a problem keeping pace with his group or grade level. When, and if, those expressions should be applied, they should be only in regard to a student's own potential. Progress should be charted by comparing a student's ability with his progress along the sequence of curricular objectives. Progress should not be gauged by comparing students with normative curricular standards.

In order to break down the lock-step nature of the curriculum, the sequence of objectives it contains should be separated from grade levels and average pace of instruction. Instead of placing one level of instructional material in a classroom, several levels, that actually match students instructional needs, should be placed there. The materials should be organized, not by grade levels, but according to the objectives for individual students in each grade. The reorganization of materials according to individual levels, rather than grade levels, would do far more to improve individualized instruction than any architectural change ever could.

Record Keeping

If the curriculum is assigned to individual students, and teaching material is available to cover a wide range of instructional levels; then a method of record keeping that matches the two is necessary. Progress for individual students will need to be plotted along the list of curricular objectives for each subject area. The record keeping procedures should relate curricular progress to the instructional materials that relate to each objective.

Progress along the curriculum is noted by what has been mastered as well as what is being learned. This procedure not only is used to insure that the match between student and instructional material is being made, but it also is the essential information for meaningful reports of pupil progress. What a student is working on and what they have mastered is the most meaningful information that can be provided to a parent or to another teacher.

CBA demands that scores on routine tests and performance on daily activities indicate a good match between student and instruction has been made. Consequently, scores produced by instructional activity will be in the same ranges for all the students in the class. Scores alone, then, will not have meaning. They can only have meaning in regard to specific curricular objectives.

Standard record keeping is used for the purpose of assigning grades. CBA record keeping is used for maintaining an instructional match. When the record book for a group of students shows a wide range of scores and grades, it indicates that only a single level of instruction is available. The variation in scores and grades shows only how variable the students are in regard to this level of instruction. In CBA, the levels of instruction must vary in order to produce the same scores, which show that accurate matches have been made. The "standard" form of record keeping must change considerably to permit curriculum-based assessment.

Grading

In the previous section on record keeping, the problem with the conventional grading system was described. In fact, if curriculum-based assessment is implemented it is impossible to produce the variance in performance that is necessary to assign a range of grades. If the use of grades were continued, then all the grades would be close to the same, and they would provide no information in regard to achievement. A teacher who used CBA, and continued reporting letter grades, would surely be accused of grade inflation.

Grades, in most places, should be replaced by a direct statement of curricular progress. If parents want to know how their child is doing relative to others in his class or age group, then the teacher can provide norm-referenced test scores, or compare the position of their child to others in his class on the sequence of curricular objectives.

Teacher Evaluation

If teacher evaluation were directed to the main components of CBA, it would naturally encourage CBA implementation. Effective teacher performance, in a classroom where CBA is used, requires a somewhat different standard than any of those now typically used.

If a teacher is using CBA, the time spent in large group instruction will be reduced. Much more time will be devoted to supervised study activities. Individual and small group activities will be going on simultaneously. Peer tutoring can be used more extensively. More time will be used to check over assignments and work with the students. The teacher will spend far less time in front of the class lecturing and demonstrating. The teacher's lesson plans will reflect multiple levels of activity. Lesson plans will be evaluated for attention to matching rather than for how well they conform to some prescribed format that usually only discourages multilevel instruction.

The evaluation procedure for teachers needs to focus on the priorities of CBA. The first thing that should be determined is if there is an accurate match between instructional activity and student. Are the students being given work that they can do. Evidence for this can be gained from direct observation in the classroom and by examining classroom records. The behavior that directly suggests that the match has been made is time-on-task. Academically engaged time should be considerably greater than in the typical classroom and is some evidence that a good match is being made. The records and lesson plans should clearly show that the students are being given work that matches their achievement level.

Examination of work done by the students and observation of work being done will show a high level of performance and comprehension for all students. The work will be at a variety of levels, but the performance will be similar. An evaluation procedure will be a part of all instructional activity.

Pupil progress should be checked, but progress should be checked in regard to what a student's potential for achievement is and where he was when he entered the teachers room. Progress should be viewed in regard to eliminating discrepancies between achievement and potential for achievement. No teacher should feel penalized by having slower or handicapped students in her or his room. This is one cause of considerable resistance to teacher evaluation based on student performance.

Testing Programs

There are important means for determining the effectiveness of teachers and schools other than tests. At the secondary level, the dropout rate is one. If students experience success and achievement, they are far more likely to stay in school. Schools and school systems very widely culturally and socioeconomically. A low dropout rate and high employment rate for graduates of one school are as important measures of effectiveness as high SAT scores with high college attendance are for another.

Some administrative policy on testing that would foster effectiveness in regard to the above, and promote CBA are: First, achievement test information should be used to insure that all students were provided instruction that matched their current level of functioning. This would be only a general gauge to be sure, but it would encourage individual attention to student needs. Second, measures of academic potential would be used to detect and prevent the emergence of a discrepancy between a student's potential and his achievement. Students with a significant achievement/potential discrepancy would receive immediate diagnostic and remedial attention. Third, there should be a policy that directs teachers to make the routine assessment be used for matching students with instructional materials. Finally, tests on student performance would be used for teacher evaluation, testing if the students of a particular teacher were doing as well as they should, not testing to compare the performance of the teacher's students to grade level standards.

Handling Mainstreamed Students

Public Law 94-142, The Education for All Handicapped Children Act, requires that handicapped students be educated with their non-handicapped peers whenever practicable. Mildly handicapped students are the most likely to be affected by this aspect of the law which has come to be called "mainstreaming."

The prospect of having a handicapped student placed in one's room has caused considerable anxiety in regular classroom teachers. Actually, most mildly handicapped children are classed as learning disabled and do not have teaching learning requirements that vary greatly from the lower achieving students who are already in the classroom. If a teacher is adequately managing the individual differences in her or his room, then the problem posed by these new students should not be particularly great. However, no handicapped student should ever be placed in the room of a teacher who does not willingly accept him. These children should not be meted out in a random fashion or even in ways that are intended to be equitable to teachers. These students should be readily accepted, if the placement is to be beneficial.

As has been stressed throughout this book, most mildly handicapped students are actually curriculum casualties. Their primary educational need is for appropriate instructional level placement. Teachers who are willing to accept these students and who have demonstrated the ability to provide to the instructional level needs of the students already in their rooms, are candidates for taking handicapped students.

On the surface this may seem to be an imposition on those teachers who are doing good work. The exceptional ability to manage to teach to the different instructional levels of a classroom full of students is the most important characteristic of good teachers. In fact, these are the primary abilities of the master teacher. This ability should be the primary component of teacher evaluation, and when identified, it should be rewarded. So, as a form of reward, or merit pay; I would suggest that when a handicapped student is placed in this exceptional teacher's room, a salary bonus accompany him. Both student and teacher would, in this way, benefit from this teacher's skill, and mainstreaming would not be considered a burden. It might go along way in helping to make handicapped students become better accepted.

Summary

Curriculum-based assessment ultimately must be practiced by the individual classroom teacher, because it involves the routine of daily instruction. Nevertheless, there are some powerful administrative tools that can be applied to encourage its practice. If curricular material were distributed in multilevels as needed within classrooms, it would not only be readily available for use by the children that need it, but it would also legitimize the idea that it is alright to work at a variety of levels within one grade. A system of record keeping that showed the match between student instructional level and the actual level of instruction being provided would keep individual differences before the teachers' eyes, constantly. It would also require that a student's progress be reported by his own appropriate level of achievement progress. The practice of grading should be modified by using reports of progress and achievement in place of letter grades. The use of letter grades fosters single level instruction in order to produce a range of grades. This practice should be curtailed. Finally, teacher evaluation procedures that value the features of CBA would certainly encourage its implementation, and it certainly would do so if effective use of CBA were monitarily rewarded.

CHAPTER 11

TEACHER TRAINING

CHARLES H. HARGIS AND SUSAN BENNER

MUCH ATTENTION is currently being devoted to American education. The specific focus of this attention has recently shifted to the training of teachers. First, the report of The Holmes Group appeared (1986), and then the report of The Carnegie Forum on Education and the Economy (1986). The quality of teacher education programs has been questioned, and some general recommendations for improvement have been proposed. One notion very clearly emerges from these reports; if there are to be changes and improvements in American education, then the changes must begin with the training of teachers.

It is also clear, that if curriculum-based assessment methods are to be incorporated in the recommended changes in education, then these concepts and methods must become a part of teacher training. This chapter is devoted to procedures for doing that.

Coursework

CBA is so much a part of the instructional process that it is not best presented as a single course. It has components that are important considerations for the history and philosophy of education, psychological foundations, curriculum design and development, and methods courses.

The concept of success is neglected in our philosophy, but a foundation point in CBA. The notion of "survival of the fittest" has been subtly pervasive in our educational system. Many teachers develop the philosophical position that failure is not only necessary, but often is good for the student. Therefore, the child, who at age six, happens to be not quite ready developmentally to read will, only learn of his own inadequacies

103

through his failure to learn to read. Teachers should be trained to maintain a success-based curriculum. Failure is unnecessary.

Currently, traditional instruction in curriculum design and development focuses on the subject matter that is to be taught. Oftentimes, curriculum development is done with little or no information regarding the individual students who will be receiving that curriculum. Once the curriculum is established, students are united with it. Sometimes this union is a successful one. At other times the curriculum and the student do not fit. Students are simply cycled through the same material in the same manner with little or no adjustment made to the student's curriculum. This cycling is repeated until the total failure and frustration is reached, at which point a special education referral may be made. Using curriculum-based instructional procedures, such a pattern will be avoided. If the teacher has the ability to make curricular adjustments as success rates fall, s/he will have maintained the child in a successful, albeit different, curriculum. While a special education program might be appropriate for such a student, it should not be mandatory that he fail, and fail repeatedly, before being allowed to enter special education. It is better that the curriculum suffer the repeated set-backs and failures rather than the student. When student teachers are in curriculum design classes, how and when to adjuct the curriculum for their students must be included in the course. The most appropriate benchmark should become the student's success rate. Rosenshine (1983) has reported that initial learning is most effective with an 80 percent success rate and that independent practice is most effective with 90 percent success rate. Thus, it becomes necessary for teachers to have a very specific notion of their objectives. As teachers are taught to monitor student progress in such a specific manner, their awareness of success rates will increase. There will be no surprise on tests, "Oh, and I thought that they knew this material." Teachers should be taught to perceive daily assignments as "test" of the match between curriculum and student (rather than tests of students). Linking curriculum design and development courses with a field experience or student teaching will facilitate the development of such skills. As long as a teacher's objective in teaching is to have students learn, and she understands that success is more effective than failure in learning, she will strive to avoid failure through curriculum adjustment just as she would use safety rules to avoid injury on the playground.

Better treatment of individual differences should be included in educational psychology courses. Quite naturally, the course on educational assessment should prominently feature assessment that is curriculum based.

Record keeping is the important tie that keeps students on their personal curricular tracks. It is necessary to effectively coordinate instructional level material to individual students. It is also the basis for reporting pupil progress. Students need detailed attention, so the topic does also.

Instruction in how to monitor and chart student success rates needs to be covered. Traditional grading systems will have to be reviewed, as they are incompatible with instruction which strives to avoid failure. When teachers maintain high success rates for their students, grade inflation becomes a problem. Misinterpretation of these high grades would result. Therefore adjustments to the traditional systems of reporting and quantifying grades must become a part of the implementation of curriculum-based assessment. Teacher education will have to provide the arena for discussion of such concepts of gradeless progress reports for elementary students, adjusted grade calculations for secondary students, and grade inflation.

Considering the controversy surrounding the use of grades (Milton, Pollio, and Eison, 1986) it would seem that it would not be so neglected a topic in teacher training programs. The use of grades and methods of reporting student progress is a practical persisting problem for teachers. It needs both theoretical and practical attention in teacher training.

Behavior management is a widely required area of study in teacher training programs. The emphasis on the management of behavior should shift to the management of instructional material and classroom organization. At least as much attention to this type of management is important. The organization of the materials and instructional activities not only greatly affect behavior, but also directly affect achievement.

In the monograph, *Effective Schooling Practice: A Research Synthesis* (Nrel, undated), one of the conclusions drawn from the research was that one of the characteristics of effective classrooms is smooth, efficient classroom routines. Organization and management of a classroom can have a direct effect on academic learning time (Arlin, 1979). Structuring of physical space, planning classroom rules, monitoring student work and behavior, and planning for feedback to students can influence student achievement. If a teacher is engaged in resolving disruptions that result from poor organization, s/he is unavailable for interactive teaching.

Because we feel that assessment is such an important part of instruction, we might even recommend a name change for all of the traditional methods courses. For example, instead of using the title, "Methods of

Teaching Reading," we might recommend, "Curriculum-Based Assessment and Instruction in Reading." The same change would hold true for math, science, social studies, and even physical education. This recommendation is a little tongue-in-cheek, but titles and labels do influence their referent, and the name shows how important this component is. Teacher education students should be taught, the value of success oriented learning, to match the curriculum to individual student levels, to monitor progress on a daily basis (including success rates for all children), and to adjust the curriculum when success rates begin to fall.

The organization of instructional material to deal with many instructional levels is a complex task. To provide for the different kinds of activities that must go on is also difficult. Alternative approaches to traditional grouping, such as peer tutoring, and cooperative learning (Slavin, 1980) are used by effective teachers. The use of such techniques can dramatically increase academic learning time. At any given time, supervised study, peer tutoring, and small group activities can be going on.

The coordination of materials with the student and activity is a considerable management problem, and it is generally more important to the management of behavior than is direct attention to behavior. Additional considerations in this management area extend into the coordination of homework to classroom work and the use of teaching devices, especially the use of computers.

Field Experience

The skills necessary to use CBA will only emerge with practice in its application. The recommended format for field experience moves from highly controlled simulation activities, and finally to the gradual takeover of a classroom.

The instruction/assessment approach which is the primary characteristic of CBA is handled through this gradual transition format. First is the opportunity to work with individual students, then small groups, and finally managing an entire class.

The length of participation is managed gradually also. First, the intern is responsible only for single periods, then longer and longer units of time.

As the field experiences enlarge, so must the intern's demonstrated level of competency. The intern teacher should not move on until s/he has demonstrated mastery of the preceding step.

The amount of time required at each level can be quite varied. For example, the basic proficiency for assessment in reading is learned best in simulation activities. An intern learns to evaluate in reading by viewing and/or listening to tapes of children reading at a variety of levels and with a variety of problems. Proficiency is determined by checking the accuracy and efficiency an intern attains in scoring taped reading activities. This is however, a fundamental skill, and interns should not begin working directly with children until this skill has been acquired.

Further, an intern should not prepare lessons for real students until s/he has reliably demonstrated skill in preparing activities for students that have been assessed through simulation. The integration of assessment with instruction will proceed in small stages with increasingly larger groups and over increasing amounts of time. The process should not be limited to prescribed time periods; it should move in coordination with emerging skill.

Supervising Teachers

The most influential component of an internship is the supervising teacher. They need to be selected carefully, and certainly rewarded appropriately. We recommend adjunct or joint appointments for these master teachers in the teacher training program. If possible, these teachers should receive merit or bonus pay for their participation.

Teachers are the critical models, and certainly in the internship experiences the models should be the best possible. The skills most valued are those that center on the delivery of instruction to classrooms of children with great individual variability. They are the assessment and management skills that permit success and achievement in each student. There are no curriculum casualties in the instructional domains of these teachers.

Material Proofing Teachers

Commercially prepared instructional materials increasingly dominate the content of curricula. They also have come to dominate even the form of the instructional activity used to reach the objectives they delineate. In what is at times called "teacher proof" materials all the activities are orchestrated, even as to what specific words the teacher is to use. Teachers are to behave according to the formula described in the teacher's manual. It is comforting for a teacher to know exactly how to perform minute-by-minute, day-by-day. Also ready-made material with attractive formats can save lots of labor. Further, materials are vested with enormous amounts of credibility. After all, they were prepared by "experts" in the field. But, the prescribed use of commercially made material has one supreme limitation; it fosters instruction to the group. Teachers must be made more material proof or material resistant. They should not let commercially available material dominate the form of their instructional activity.

There is a great deal of good to be said about some of this material, but teachers must learn to control the delivery of instruction according to the variety of needs that exist in the classroom. This will be done when they use assessment information, taken directly from individual students, to select appropriate instructional level activities and materials. Asssessment should dictate the type of material and the form of instruction. Teachers in training need a great deal of practice doing this very thing.

Summary

At the beginning of the chapter, we mentioned the criticism teacher training was receiving. The defects pointed out are varied and often not particularly specific. The recommended changes are also considerable, but are directed to the general nature of teacher training. Nationwide, changes in teacher training are occurring to meet these general recommendations. There remain, however, skeptical critics such as Baird W. Whitlock (1986) who suggest that individual can't really be taught pedagogy, and that good teacher education programs are not possible. Of course we believe this view is not true at all, but we do feel that what makes a teacher competent is not what we typically think of as pedagogy. The pervasive notion of what makes good pedagogy, or teaching, is often confused with obvious, even pedantic, qualities. (This may be due at least in some part to the fact the primary model of teaching has been provided by college professors.) Our view is that the fundatmentals of good teaching are made up of quality assessment, accounting, and management practices. These are the ingredients of CBA and are essential, especially at the elementary school level. CBA does not seem particularly pedagogical. Nonetheless, we feel its practice should be among the minimum basal skills of the teachers of the future. The practice of CBA should be evidence of minimal competence. It is the journeyman's test, so-to-speak.

Good teaching and good teachers can be made up of many and diverse things, but they are all in addition to the CBA skills. Given adequate aptitude, the elements and skills that comprise CBA are teachable and learnable. The other qualities that make a good teacher outstanding are secondary. Only after CBA becomes standard practice should they be the focus of educational thought and research.

REFERENCES

Arlin, M. (1979). Teacher transitions can disrupt time flow in classrooms. *American Educational Research Journal, 16,* 42-56.

Ashlock, R. B. (1986). *Error patterns in computation* (4th ed.). Columbus: Merrill.

Betts, E. A. (1936). *The prevention and correction of reading difficulties.* Evanston: Row Peterson.

Betts, E. A. (1946). *Foundations of reading instruction.* New York: American Book.

Carnegie Forum on Education and the Economy. (1986). *A nation prepared: Teachers for the 21st century.* New York: Author.

Dolch, E. W. (1941). *Teaching primary reading.* Champaign: Garrard.

Forell, E. R. (1985). The case for conservative reader placement. The Reading Teacher, 38, 857-862.

Gagne, R. M. (1970). Some new views of learning. *Phi Delta Kappan, 51,* 468-472.

Gates, A. I. (1930). *Interest and ability in reading.* New York: Macmillan.

Gickling, E., Hargis, C. H., and Alexander, D. R. (1981). The funciton of imagery in sight word recognition among retarded and nonretarded children. *Education and Training of the Mentally Retarded, 16,* 259-263.

Gickling, E. and Thompson, V. (1985). A personal view of curriculum-based assessment. *Exceptional Children, 52,* 205-218.

Grimes, L., (1981). Learned helplessness and attribution theory: Redefining children's learning problems. *Learning Disability Quarterly, 4,* 91-100.

Hallahan, D. P. ad Kauffman, J. M. (1986). *Exceptional Children* (3rd ed.). Englewood Cliffs: Prentice-Hall.

Hargis, C. H. (1985, November). *Word introduction and repetition rates.* Paper presented at the 11th Southeastern IRA regional Conference, Nashville, TN.

Hargis, C. H. (1982). *Teaching reading to Handicapped children.* Denver: Love.

Hargis, C. H. (1978, July). *Word recognition development as a function of imagery level.* Paper presented at the summer meeting of the Linguistic Society of America, Champaign-Urbana.

Hargis, C. H., and Gickling, E. E. (1978). The function of imagery in word recognition development. *The Reading Teacher, 32,* 570-574.

Harris, A. J., and Sipay, E. R. (1975). *How to increase reading ability* (6th ed.). New York: David McKay.

The Holmes Group. (1986). *Tomorrows teachers: a report of the Holmes Group.* East Lansing, MI: Author.

Jansky, J., and de Hirsch, K. (1972). *Preventing reading failure: Prediction, diagnosis, intervention.* New York: Harper and Row.

Jenkins, J. R., and Pany, D. (1978). Standardized achievement tests: How useful for special education? *Exceptional Children, 44,* 448-453.

Loftus, E. F., and Suppes, P. (1972). Structural variables that determine problem-solving difficulty in computer-assisted instruction. *Journal of Educational Psychology, 63,* 531-542.

Mangieri, J., and Kahn, M. S. (1977). Is the Dolch list of 220 words irrelevant? *Reading Teacher, 30,* 649-651.

Miller, G. A. (1956). The magical number seven, plus or minus two. *Psychological Review, 63,* 81-97.

Milton, O., Pollio, H. R., and Eison, J. A. (1986). *Making sense of college grades.* San Francisco: Jossey-Bass.

Resnick, L. B. , and Ford, W. W. (1981). *The psychology of mathematics for instruction.* Hillsdale: Lawrence Erlbaum.

Northwest Regional Education Laboratory. (undated). *Effective schooling practices: A research synthesis.* Portland Oregon: NREL.

Rosenshine, B. V., and Berliner, D. C. (1978). Academic engaged time. *British Journal of Teacher Education, 4,* 3-16.

Rosenshine, B. (1983). Teaching functions in instructional programs. *Elementary School Journal, 83,* 335-351.

Skinner, B. F. (1972). Teaching: The arrangement of contingencies under which something is taught. In N. G. Haring and A. H. Hayden (Eds.), *Improvement of instruction,* Seattle: Special Child.

Slavin, R. (1980). Cooperative learning. *Review of Educational Research, 50,* 317-343.

Spache, G. D. (1976). *Diagnosing and correcting reading disabilities,* Boston: Allyn and Bacon.

Spache, G. D. (1976). *Investigating the issues of reading disabilities.* Boston: Allyn and Bacon.

Spache, G. D. (1972). *Diagnostic Reading Scales.* Monterey: California Test Bureau.

Thompson, V. P., Gickling, E. E., and Havertape, J. F. (1983). The effects of medication and curriculum on task-related behaviors of attention deficit disordered and low achieving peers. *Monographs in behavioral disorders: Severe behavior disorders of children and youth.* CCBD, Arizona State University. Series #6.

Tucker, J. A. (1985). Curriculum-based assessment: An introduction. *Exceptional Children, 52,* 199-204.

Whitlock, B. W. (1986). *Educational myths I have known and loved.* New York: Schocken Books.

INDEX

A

Arithmetic assessment, 59-62
Arlin, M., 105
Ashlock, R., 61

B

Berliner, D., 34
Betts, E., 4, 31, 51, 52, 54

C

Carnegie Forum on Education and the Economy, 103
Concreteness, 48, 59 (*see also* Imagery)
Curriculum casualties, 4, 82

D

De Hirsch, K., 5
Diagnostic Reading Scales, 26
Direct assessment, 51, 65-66
Dolch Basic Sight Word List, 36

E

Eison, J., 105

F

Failure, 3-6, 9-12, 16, 19, 24, 25, 89-91
  avoiding, 19
  off-task behavior, 24
  predicting, 16
  whose fault, 11
  why it fails, 10
  why it is required, 9
Field experience, 106, 107
Ford, W., 46, 48
Forell, E., 9, 11
Frustration level, 67

G

Gagne, R., 45
Gates, A., 30, 31, 35, 73, 75
Gickling, E., 34, 36, 44, 83
Grades, 10

Grading, 5, 91, 97, 98, 100, 101
Grimes, L., 11
Group instruction, 95, 96

H

Hallahan, D., 81
Hargis, C., 10, 36, 38
Harris, A., 5
Havertape, J., 83
Hewitt, F., 82
Holmes Group, 103

I

Imagery, 35, 36
Independent reading level, 33, 34, 51, 52
Individual differences, 4, 6, 14
Informal reading inventory, 52-55
Instructional level, 20, 24, 25, 51, 52, 65, 70
  in arithmetic, 43-50
  in reading, 29-41
Instruction with assessment, 51-63

J

Jansky, J., 5
Jenkins, J., 16

K

Kauffman, J., 81
Kirk, S., 81

L

Learning disabled, 3, 5, 7, 12, 18, 36, 39, 49, 81-85
  curriculum casualties, 82
  identification of, 81-85
Lock step curriculum, 4
Loftus, E., 46
Low achievers, 5, 7, 9, 12, 18, 36, 39, 49

M

Mangieri, J., 36
Meaningfulness, 48, 49

113

Miller, G., 44, 77
Milton, O., 105

O

Off-task behavior, 24, 27
On-task time, 5

P

Pany, D., 16
Pollio, H., 105
Procrustus, 3, 63
Proficiency tests, 88

R

Radford, D., 36
Readiness, 46, 76
Record keeping, 96, 97, 100, 105
Reliability, 17
Remedial instruction, 78, 79
Repetition, 69, 73, 74, 76
  practice, 77
  drill, 77
Repetition rates
  accuracy in, 76
  in arithmetic, 45-50
  in reading, 34-41
Resnik, L., 46, 48
Rosenshine, B., 34, 104

S

Scores 27, 43, 51, 92, 93
  maintaining the same scores, 28, 43
  uniformity of, 43
Sipay, E., 5
Skinner, B., 82
Slavin, R., 106
Spache, G., 4, 53
Success, 5, 6, 9, 11, 12
  insuring, 27
  scores for, 13
Supervising teachers, 107
Suppes, P., 46

T

Testing and teaching, 30
Tests
  case history, 19
  criterion-referenced, 17, 18
  curriculum-referenced, 17, 20, 21
  diagnostic, 18, 19
  IQ, 87, 89
  norm-referenced, 17, 27
  proficiency, 21, 22
  purposes of, 89-93
  readiness, 16, 19, 20
  reading capacity, 25, 26
  reading-readiness, 17
  relevance, 21-23
  screening, 18
  subskills, 22, 23
  teaching of, 22, 26
Teacher evaluation, 98, 99
Teacher proof materials, 107, 108
Theseus, 3
Thompson, V., 34, 44, 83
Tucker, J., 26

V

Validity, 5
  content, 15, 22
  criterion related, 16
  curriculum-based tests, 16
  predictive, 16

W

Whitlock, B., 108
Word calling, 38
Word identification, 37, 38, 40, 74-76
Word-identification skills
  assessment of 56-59
Word problems, 50
Word recognition, 37, 38